Pitt Series in Policy and Institutional Studies

HOMEWARD BOUND

HOMEWARD BOUND
Explaining Changes in Congressional Behavior

GLENN R. PARKER

University of Pittsburgh Press

Published by the University of Pittsburgh Press, Pittsburgh, PA 15260
Copyright © 1986, University of Pittsburgh Press
All rights reserved
Feffer and Simons, Inc., London
Manufactured in the United States of America

Library of Congress Cataloging-in-Publication Data

Parker, Glenn R.
  Homeward bound.

  (Pitt series in policy and institutional studies)
  Bibliography: p. 195
  Includes index.
  1. United States. Congress—Constituent
communication.   2. United States. Congress.
I. Title.   II. Series.
JK1140.P37   1986   328.73'07331   86-4098
ISBN 0-8229-3536-8

To S.L.P.
a constant source of inspiration and support

Contents

Figures

Tables

Preface

An infrequently examined arena of congressional behavior is the constituency. It is an arena where incumbents spend a lot of time and where members' activities can affect what they do or cannot do in Washington. The interrelationship between activities at home and in Washington makes the study of behavior with regard to the constituency an important contribution to the understanding of legislative behavior. In this book I examine the relationship between home and Washington activities, the ways in which it has changed over time, and the reasons for this change. In order to do this, I analyze a component of the home styles of House and Senate incumbents—how they allocate their personal time to constituency affairs. Richard Fenno (1978) first coined the term *home style* to describe the ways in which incumbents cultivate their constituencies. Fenno suggested that House incumbents were paying more attention to their constituents today than in the past; a major objective of my inquiry is to explain why incumbents have adopted more attentive home styles. Specifically, this study addresses three questions: When did the adoption of attentive home styles occur? Why did congressmen and senators adopt attentive styles? And what institutional consequences have the widespread adoption of attentive home styles had?

The argument is advanced that changes have occurred in the behavior of congressmen and senators toward their constituencies since the mid-1960s: they are placing a greater emphasis on service to the district or state. This change in home styles was facilitated by Congress in its efforts to accommodate members' needs for electoral safety, services to constituents, and political leeway from control by the constituency. Congress accomplished this by reducing the costs associated with attention to the constituency. In the process, incentives for members to adopt more attentive home styles were established. The widespread conversion of older members to higher levels of attentiveness and the adoption of attentive home styles on the part of new members enhanced electoral safety and enabled incumbents to pursue other legislative goals, such as power and influence on policy. The pursuit of these personal legislative goals increased the individuality of congressmen and senators and fostered further dispersions of power within Congress.

Two characteristics of this inquiry are particularly important to an understanding of home-style changes: the bicameral focus and the longitudinal analysis. House-Senate comparisons of the factors promoting the adoption of attentive styles and the consequences of their widespread adoption broaden understanding of how and why home styles change. Institutional differences can be linked to differences in the nature and structure of the House and Senate; likewise, similarities can be linked to common precipitating factors and similar institutional responses. The longitudinal study of home-style change is important because it provides a historical context for understanding the dynamics of change. Joseph Cooper and David Brady (1981) have argued that such diachronic approaches to congressional behavior have an advantage over most static studies of institutional behavior because they integrate the historical context into explanations of behavior change. The resulting explanations specify interrelationships among historical conditions, individual behaviors, and institutional structures. In this study, the explanation for the adoption of attentive home styles involves changes in institutional characteristics, members' goals, and electoral conditions. The inclusion of historical conditions in the explanation of change in home style increases the breadth of the generalizations drawn and reduces the likelihood that the findings are time-bound or are artifacts of particular periods or congresses.

Three common methods for examining change in behavior are

used in analyzing changes in attention: cohort, panel, and time-series analyses. In isolating individual generations of congressmen and senators for study, one is able to generalize about the effects associated with individual cohorts and periods over a series of cross-sectional samples. With panel data, repeated measurements of a particular behavior or attitude of the same individual provide a means for analyzing individual change. Time-series analysis identifies the causal dynamics underlying a series of observations taken at regular intervals over time. This inquiry incorporates each of these approaches into the study of home-style changes: cohort analysis is used to determine when and why home styles change; panel analysis provides evidence of individual changes and their effects on electoral safety; time-series analysis is used to examine the impact of institutional changes on changes in attentiveness over time. This multimethod approach broadens knowledge of changes in home style since each approach contributes a different perspective on change and its effects.

In chapter 1, I describe the general contours of the analysis and the major questions examined, and in chapter 2, I examine the stability of home styles and the extent to which individual circumstances induce changes in attention to constituency. I also describe the measurement of attention to constituency and change in style. The effects of institutional and societal forces on change in home style are analyzed in chapter 3. Attention is given to the impact of increased travel subsidies, career-cycle emphases, and generational differences in styles in explaining changes in aggregate levels of attention to the constituency. In chapter 4, I examine the immediate and long-term effects of changes in the costs of attention and evaluate the impact of institutional incentives that reduce the costs of attentiveness on the day-to-day attention of members to their constituents. In chapter 5, I analyze the role of attention and changes in style in generating electoral safety for House and Senate incumbents. Chapter 6 is devoted to a discussion of the direct and indirect consequences of changes in home style for the functioning of Congress.

Acknowledgments

I would like to acknowledge the support of the National Science Foundation (grant SES-8217489) and the Florida State University throughout this study; without this support, my efforts would have fallen far short of my goals. I would also like to acknowledge the assistance of several scholars: Roger H. Davidson and Bert Rockman for their insightful remarks and suggestions regarding the manuscript; Joseph Cooper, Richard Fenno, and Morris Fiorina for the advice and assistance that they provided throughout the inquiry; Stephanie Larson for her diligence and care in collecting and coding the data; Mary Schneider for typing the manuscript; and Suzanne Parker for unselfishly giving scholarly attention to each chapter and for serving as a critical and captive audience for many of the ideas contained in this book. None of these sources of advice or assistance, however, bear any responsibility for the statements or conclusions made in this work.

HOMEWARD BOUND

: 1 :

Introduction

THE INDEPENDENCE OF MEMBERS

A salient characteristic of the modern Congress, if not earlier ones, is the individuality of its members. Congressman Herman Eberharter's admonishment to Lewis Dexter (1977, p. 5) as he began his research for *American Business and Public Policy* (Bauer, Pool, and Dexter, 1963) in the early 1950s—"I am sure you will find out a congressman can do pretty much what he decides to do"—is as accurate today as it was then. "What is important to each congressman, and vitally so, is that he be free to take positions that serve his advantage. There is no member of either house who would not be politically injured—or at least who would not think he would be injured—by being made to toe the party line on all policies (unless of course he could determine the line)" (Mayhew, 1974a, p. 88). A clever lexicon has even been developed to convey succinctly the image of Congress as an institution of individuals; hence the House is characterized as a collection of 435 "small" businesses (Loomis, 1979) or member "enterprises" (Salisbury and Shepsle, 1981), and the Senate is described as a "hundred barons" (Matthews, 1973, p. 118). Whatever the characterization, the same impression emerges: Congress is populated by fiercely independent legislators who exercise unusual discretion over their own actions.

It is useful to view the independence or autonomy of legislators at different times as falling along a continuum, extending from positions of little independence to positions of total autonomy. From this perspective, one can speak of congressmen and senators as becoming more or less independent, and one can associate these changes with certain situational factors or conditions that promote or impede such autonomy. There are at least five factors that have bolstered the independence of congressmen and senators, four of which have been discussed extensively in the literature on Congress: the decline of the importance of party, membership changes, the organization of Congress, and the institutionalization of the House and Senate. To this list I would add another factor: the adoption of attentive home styles. Simply put, behavioral changes on the part of congressmen and senators enabled them to free themselves from the pressures of constituency. It is this topic—change in style among congressmen and senators—that serves as the focus of this study, but before I analyze the adoption of attentive home styles, I will describe how the other four factors have enhanced the independence of members.

The Decline of Party

By now, most congressional scholars are familiar with David Broder's somewhat prophetic lament that "the party's over" (1971). And, indeed, the symptoms of the decline of party seem to be everywhere: the rise in split-ticket voting (Ornstein et al., 1982, p. 53), the virtual disappearance of presidential coattails as an electoral force (Kritzer and Eubank, 1979), and the growth in the use of incumbency as a voting cue in Senate (Kostroski, 1973) and House (Ferejohn, 1977) elections. The decline in the electoral importance of political parties freed members from the constraints imposed by party discipline and the pressures of their leaders. Joseph Cooper and David Brady argue that the capacity of legislative leaders to exercise meaningful control over their colleagues was undermined by the fragmentation in the party system that resulted from the emergence of divisive partisan issues. "If it is true that factionalism in the party system led to the decline of party control mechanisms, it is also true that the decline of these mechanisms had the further effect of allowing party factionalism greater expression. The result of these developments was to heighten the power and independence of the individual member and of key organizational units in the House" (Cooper and Brady, 1981, p. 417).

Whatever the cause of the declining relevance of party, incumbents responded by developing personal followings to buffer their electoral margins against the erosion in partisanship; as these personal followings grew, partisan loyalty became less central to victory. With declining dependence upon the political party for electoral support, members were less susceptible to leadership pressures. Party support had to be bargained for rather than commanded. Thus the decline of party as an electoral force has bolstered the capacity and willingness of congressmen and senators to ignore partisan pleas and discipline, unless it suits their own designs. "It seems plain that the decay of electoral parties and the growing independence of voters have their counterpart in Congress: . . . legislators who can take party or leave it, knowing that the only masters they must serve are their renomination and reelection constituencies" (Keefe, 1980, p. 11).

Membership Changes

Perhaps the most obvious reason for the individuality exhibited by members in the modern Congress is that the institution has attracted a different type of congressman and senator. Not only are members entering Congress at an earlier age than in the past, but they also appear to be more ambitious than past cohorts (Payne, 1980). Both factors are apt to reduce their willingness to follow their leaders. Writing about the individualism of legislators during the 1970s, James Sundquist characterizes the type of member entering Congress in these terms: "Junior members will accept leadership only on their own terms, and subject to their continuous control. They insist on the right to decide day by day and case by case, without coercion, when they will be followers and when they will assert their right of independence" (Sundquist, 1981, p. 391). In short, the election of more independent-minded legislators has created an institutional environment where political individuality prospers and party discipline flounders.

The Organization of Congress

There are some organizational features of Congress itself that have contributed to the independence of its members (Froman, 1968;

Cooper, 1981). For example, the widespread decentralization of legislative power within Congress has provided members with vantage points to counter the influence and pressures of their leaders. At the very least, the decentralization of influence makes leaders hesitant about applying too much pressure for fear of a reaction that thwarts leadership designs at some future date; an offended subcommittee leader could conceivably endanger the plans of party leaders. Other organizational attributes, such as the lack of tolerance for hierarchy (Cooper, 1981), also bolster the independence of congressmen and senators by setting constraints on the exercise of leadership.

Another feature of the organizational terrain of Congress that reinforces the independence of its members is the existence of norms—unwritten codes of behavior and conduct. Norms, like specialization (members are expected to concentrate on a narrow set of interests), elevate the expertise of members to the point where they can serve as alternative cues for voting on policy matters; the expertise of these individuals certainly makes their arguments as compelling as those advanced by congressional leaders, if not more so. The specialization norm also requires that leaders formulate their policies with an eye toward what is acceptable to their experts within the party; in this way, policy-making influence is further decentralized. Thus the organization of Congress has enhanced the influence of most members vis-à-vis their leaders and, in the process, provided incumbents with more opportunities to exercise legislative leadership themselves. The strategy of House leaders for coopting members by allowing them greater involvement in decision making (Sinclair, 1983) is one manifestation of the improved position of followers and their leverage with their leaders.

The Institutionalization of Congress

Nelson Polsby (1968) was one of the first congressional scholars to describe the trends in the development of Congress as a political institution. Polsby suggested that the institutionalization of the House, for instance, was evident in its differentiation from its external environment, its growth in internal complexity, and its adoption of automatic rather than discretionary methods for the conduct of legislative business. While all of these developments probably contributed in some way to the independence of congressmen and senators, the shift from discretionary to automatic decision rules may be the most important. As more and more decisions are based upon automatic rules, the ability of party leaders to use their position to improve a member's lot evaporates. "Sam Rayburn's advice, 'To get along, go along,' no longer needs to be taken seriously, since each member will in any case have substantial resources under his or her control and hence may get along nicely without going along at all" (Salisbury and Shepsle, 1981, p. 570).

Most of what members want, like committee assignments, have become matters of right, or at least seniority. Where leaders might have been inclined in the past to withhold benefits from members, they are now more willing to accommodate their requests in the hope of building goodwill. In the process of institutionalization, then, members have gained a measure of control over resources that were once subject to the discretion of their leaders; as a consequence, another set of resources at the disposal of leaders for engendering legislative support was stripped away. With guaranteed access to such resources, members could engage in the types of entrepreneurial activity that characterize their individuality.

The Adoption of Attentive Home Styles

The final factor that has promoted the independence of incumbents is the adoption of attentive home styles. Most of the factors that I have discussed have reduced the dependence of members on their party leaders; the adoption of attentive styles, in contrast, helped to reduce the compulsion of members to follow the dictates of their constituents. By cultivating the appearance of attentiveness and by convincing constituents that their interests are well cared for no matter what the legislator does in Washington, incumbents have gained a measure of freedom from scrutiny and interference on the part of constituents. In situations where incumbents act contrary to the prevailing opinion in their constituency, an attentive home style can mute whatever adverse reaction might arise. Simply put, the adoption of an attentive home style provided incumbents with a way of staying in office without subjugating their own policy preferences or goals to the whims of their constituents.

The adoption of attentive home styles is one of several factors that have enhanced the individuality of congressmen and senators.

We might also add that all of the factors mentioned are probably interrelated in some complex way. For instance, membership changes may be partially responsible for organizational, institutional, and home-style changes that have strengthened the legislative independence of incumbents. Or the decline of party as an electoral force may have provided the opportunities for membership changes to occur; perhaps changes in attentiveness stimulated some organizational and institutional changes that furthered the individuality of members. In short, there are probably manifold interrelationships among these five factors that are direct and/or indirect in nature. My purpose in this study is not to sort out these causal linkages, even if that were possible; rather, it is to suggest that whatever the interrelationships, changes in home style enhanced the independence of members in the same way as did the decline of party, the changes in membership, and the organization and institutionalization of Congress. I will return in chapter 6 to this question of the impact of an attentive home style on the independence of members; I turn at this point to a discussion of home style itself and why it has changed.

THE STUDY OF HOME STYLE

Our understanding of legislative behavior is largely limited to the activities of congressmen and senators as they serve in the nation's Capitol. A substantial body of literature has helped to clarify the voting behavior of members on the floor (Clausen, 1973; Kingdon, 1973; Matthews and Stimson, 1975; Fiorina, 1974) and in committees (Fenno, 1973; Parker and Parker, 1985a), the activities of party leaders (Huitt, 1961; Peabody, 1976; Ripley, 1967 and 1969; Sinclair, 1983), and the relationship between the president, his executive agencies, and members of Congress (Wildavsky, 1964; Ferejohn, 1974; Fiorina, 1977; Arnold, 1979). There is ample scholarly justification for this emphasis on the Washington-based activities of congressmen and senators since legislators in both chambers devote a large proportion of their time to these activities.

Time in Washington normally is divided between voting on the floor and fulfilling committee responsibilities. For many members, their entire days are occupied with moving between committee deliberations and floor votes. The time that is not spent on the floor or in committees is often wasted as they shuttle between their committee rooms and House and Senate chambers when the bells that identify the type of floor vote sound; at the conclusion of these votes, members return to their committees and offices and pick up where they left off before the interruption. It is easy to understand why the behavior of congressmen and senators on the floor of their respective chambers, and in their committees, has provided the context for most analyses of congressional behavior: it is the arena in which a variety of legislative activity occurs.

THE PURPOSES OF HOME STYLE

Establishment of Trust

While Washington-based activities occupy large amounts of the time of congressmen and senators, members also spend considerable time in their districts and states cultivating their constituents. Richard Fenno's studies of the home style of congressmen (1978) and senators (1982) directed attention to this neglected area of congressional research. It is this "world of the shopping bags" that Fenno sees as a critical context for the study of legislative behavior. Not only have members begun to spend considerable amounts of time in their constituencies, but such attentiveness may affect what they do (and can or cannot do) when in Washington. For instance, Fenno (1978) suggests that House incumbents are able to gain a measure of leeway in matters of policy through judicious cultivation of their congressional districts. In this sense, attention to the constituency may buy some freedom in Washington. In order to gain such latitude, legislators must be able to create an aura of trust that will permit them to express their individuality freely in their policy-making and other legislative pursuits.

Three components of home style have as their purpose the establishment of trust: (1) the allocation of resources; (2) presentation of self; and (3) explanation of Washington activity.

Allocation of Resources

Allocation of time to constituency activities poses a dilemma for most members of Congress because the time they spend in the district or state could be spent on legislative or other Washington activities. This zero-sum situation causes a strain between the need to attend to Washington business and the need to attend to constituency affairs. The way members allocate their office resources between these two responsibilities provides a basis for evaluating their degree of attentiveness to the constituency.

Of course, there is a variety of resources at the member's command, and in some cases district or state attention may "cost" an incumbent very little. For instance, sending newsletters to constituents can be delegated to staff, thereby reducing the time that a member needs to devote to Washington activities. Further, other staff members can perform the neglected legislative responsibilities without severely constraining office capabilities. Therefore, some activities place less of a drain on resources and, in such cases, the allocation decisions may not be as critical.

On the other hand, some resources are so scarce and precious that the allocative decision is viewed by members as a zero-sum situation. While the time and responsibilities of office staff can be divided between the constituency and Washington, an incumbent often finds that "when he is doing something at home, he must give up doing some things in Washington and vice versa" (Fenno, 1978, p. 34). The time that they spend in their constituencies represents the allocation of a resource so scarce and precious that this decision effectively differentiates among incumbents in terms of their attentiveness to constituency affairs. Personal attention to district or state affairs fosters the types of images that enhance constituent trust.

Presentation of Self

Time spent in the district or state provides an unusual opportunity for members to transmit messages that enhance trust on the part of constituents. According to Fenno, the centerpiece of an incumbent's home style is the presentation of self, the way in which the member relates to constituents. Fenno suggests that House incumbents are constantly attempting to project images that will engender political support and trust among constituents.

For their part, constituents must rely on trust. They must "accept on faith" that the congressman is what he says he is and will do what he says he will do. House members, for their part, are quite happy to emphasize trust. It helps to allay the uncertainties they feel about their relationship with their supportive constituencies. If members are uncertain as to how to work for support directly, they can always work indirectly to win a degree of personal trust that will increase the likelihood of support or decrease the likelihood of opposition. (Fenno, 1978, p. 56)

Many of the communications between legislators and constituents reflect this relentless effort to reinforce trust. For those members who are successful at this endeavor, electoral security and leeway in matters of policy are likely by-products.

In order to elicit trust, all congressmen attempt to create impressions that they are *qualified* to hold office; that they can *identify* with the values and attitudes of constituents; and that they can *empathize* with the problems of constituents. These messages are transmitted at every opportunity that a member has to communicate with constituents. The more personal and pervasive the contact, the greater the probability that the message will be retained; repetition is a member's insurance against being "forgotten" at election time.

Explanation of Washington Activity

The final component of a home style is the way in which members rationalize their Washington activities to their constituents. Fenno (1978) refers to this element as "explanations of Washington activities." Explanations are the mechanisms through which incumbents describe, interpret, and justify legislative pursuits, especially the two major preoccupations, power (Dodd, 1977) and policy (Fenno, 1973). The pursuit of power, for example, is often justified by claiming that such influence is used to further district or state interests.

Even though they probably have little to fear from electoral reprisals for one or two unpopular votes, senators and congressmen explain their votes and policy positions to their constituents. Most constituents lack any awareness of the specific votes cast, and most perceive their members as voting in line with constituent sentiment (Parker, 1981a). A string of "wrong" votes could pose problems (Kingdon, 1973), but most members avoid creating such patterns in their votes by developing a good sense of the policy positions that are likely to produce adverse reactions from their constituents. Since there is always some uncertainty as to what votes a member may be called upon to explain (Fenno, 1978, p. 142), members tend to stockpile more explanations than they need.

These explanations can be used by members to gain some leeway in their pursuits in Washington. Since it is impossible for constituents to keep tabs on their legislators, especially when they are in Washington, they are largely uninformed about the behavior of their congressmen and senators. This "invisibility" can be exploited by incumbents to pursue personal goals without worrying about the reactions of constituents. For example, some seek independence from the policy preferences of their constituents so that they can exercise their own judgment and promote ideologically satisfying causes. The reservoirs of trust built up through attention to the constituency enable members to exercise independence in their pursuit of personal goals. If constituents trust their representatives and senators, they are likely to grant them freedom from surveillance; that is, constituents assume that their legislator is fulfilling constituency obligations and congressional responsibilities, unless they hear otherwise.

While the actions of incumbents may be invisible to their constituents, the incumbents themselves are not. Constituents normally find their legislators willing and prepared to explain their Washington activities, and their frequent appearances in their constituencies provide ample opportunities to question them about these activities. The fact that members frequently make themselves available to constituents reinforces constituents' trust.

Qualification, identification, and empathy are all helpful in the building of constituent trust. To a large degree these three impressions are conveyed by the very fact of regular contact. That is, "I prove to you that I am qualified," or "I prove to you that I am one of you," or "I prove to you that I understand," by coming around frequently to let you see me, to see you and to meet with you. If, on the other hand, I failed to come home to see and be seen, to talk and be talked to, then you would have some reason to worry about trusting me. (Fenno, 1978, p. 60)

In short, explanations of Washington activities can quiet constituents' fears about the responsiveness of their members while in Washington, at the same time that they serve as mechanisms for generating trust.

As congressmen and senators explain their Washington behavior to their constituents, they also use these opportunities to differentiate themselves from other members of Congress. They tend to picture themselves as different from, and better than, both past and present legislators. Many constituents appear to learn this message well, as is evidenced by their tendency to see their own representatives as distinctly better than other congressmen (Parker, 1981c). In the process of promoting their own images, incumbents frequently demean and degrade the Congress: "each member of Congress polishes his or her individual reputation at the expense of the institutional reputation of Congress" (Fenno, 1978, p. 164). Attacks on Congress enable members to shed the blame for whatever national condition has soured their constituents on the legislative process. The lack of an energy policy can be attributed to the "big oil interests" that hold power in Congress, or the "outmoded committee system"; enormous budget deficits can be blamed on the "big welfare spenders" or the "hawks" in Congress, depending upon whether constituents favor social service programs or national defense appropriations. In this way, members are able to extricate themselves from the adverse conditions that produce discontent among constituents. These attacks on Congress not only are accepted by constituents as "placing the blame where it belongs" but are also likely to further endear members to their constituents, who normally are highly critical of the institution.

In sum, the home-style activities of legislators (allocation of resources, presentation of self, explanation of Washington activity) are designed to generate trust on the part of constituents. Incumbents hope to develop home styles that will create sufficient trust to permit them to pursue personal goals in Congress without fear of adverse reaction or interference from voters. Constituents willingly invest trust in their legislators when they are convinced that their members are attentive to district or state interests and are likely to sustain that level of attention in the future.

Representational Responsibilities

The home-style activities of congressmen and senators are not entirely self-serving, however, since they meet legitimate representational responsibilities. Constituents expect to be kept informed about issues that are relevant to their concerns. Members can oblige their constituents by providing such information, while also taking the opportunity to further their own popularity through these communications.

In fulfilling representational demands and satisfying constituent expectations, incumbents also are able to accomplish electoral objectives. David Mayhew (1974a), for example, identifies three activities engaged in by congressmen for the electoral opportunities they provide: advertising, credit claiming, and position taking. These activities occupy a large proportion of the messages to constituents in the congressmen's correspondence (Saloma, 1969; Yiannakis, 1982). Advertising activities are designed to disseminate the incumbents' name widely among constituents and to associate it with a positive image. They represent attempts to create the belief that incumbents are personally responsible for the particularized benefits that their constituents are receiving, such as federal support for district or state projects. While the notion of benefits generally conjures up images of the legislative pork barrel, a large proportion of the particularized benefits that members funnel to their constituents does not even involve legislative action; rather, it is the result of casework on behalf of constituents (Mayhew, 1974a, p. 55). Credit claiming attempts to create the belief that benefits to the constituency are solely attributable to the efforts of its representative. Finally, position taking reflects the efforts of incumbents to take policy stands that are pleasing to their constituents. There is no better way for members to endear themselves to constituents than by publicly voicing policy positions that are strongly supported in the district or state.

Senators, as well as representatives, avail themselves of the benefits that can be derived from elements of home style that combine electoral and representational activities. "Any inhabitant of Capitol Hill, from elevator operator to vice-president, will tell you that 'the most effective kind of campaigning is done between elections.' The incumbent senator who campaigns during the political off-season has no opponent" (Matthews, 1973, p. 228). Despite this similarity, there are significant differences between the home styles of congressmen and senators. For example, senate campaigns place a greater emphasis on the mass media and receive most of the news space that is devoted to congressional elections. Thus they are able to make use of "free information" to a greater extent than House campaigns can (Parker, 1981b; Fenno, 1982). Media coverage of House races palls in comparison for a number of reasons.

As members of the smaller of the two bodies, senators are easier to get to know and to cover than members of the larger House. The more coverage they get, the better known they become; the better known, the more coverage they attract—and so on. Since every senator will presumably be around for six years, coverage of them is a less risky investment of a journalist's time than coverage of a House member. Similarly, the internal proceedings of a group of 100 are easier to follow, record, and analyze than the proceedings of 435 . . . moreover, each senator's share of legislative power is four times as great as each representative's share. (Ibid., p. 10)

The major difference between the constituency activities of senators and congressmen has little to do with the activities that they pursue with respect to their constituencies since they generally both do the same sorts of things. They differ in the emphasis that they place on certain types of activities. For instance, senators do not feel that they can effectively reach a large number of their constituents through personal contact. Hence they do not normally spend as much time in their states as House incumbents spend in their districts (Fig. 1). Congressmen, on the other hand, feel that such contact is worthwhile and effective. Further, the media attention that senators receive ensures that senate elections contain a much greater policy component than House races. This means that "Senate candidates talk about public policy questions more than House candidates do" (ibid., p. 170). A basic cause of these differences in style between congressmen and senators is the size of the constituencies that they represent. The smaller the size differential between the state and the congressional district, the greater the similarity between the styles of House and Senate incumbents. The larger the gap in size between congressional and senate constituencies, the less the styles of congressmen and senators will resemble one another (ibid., 1982).

As this brief review illustrates, there are a variety of activities at an incumbent's disposal for developing a favorable image among constituents. Such activities not only provide flexibility in policy and personal freedom in Washington but also give members electoral opportunities that they can exploit for their own benefit. In the process, legitimate representational responsibilities are served by these activities: explanations provide constituents with information about important policies that affect them; casework gives constituents a personal link with government; district or state visits allow face-to-face contact between the representative and those represented. Ironically, these activities may also help to ensure that the incumbents are returned to office time after time.

EVIDENCE OF CHANGE

The major objectives of this book are to demonstrate that changes have occurred in the home styles of congressmen and senators and to assess the effects to those changes on Congress. (In chapter 3 an extended analysis is presented to support the assertion that aggregate changes in the home styles of congressmen and senators have occurred and to offer explanations for such changes). This section is limited to summarizing research that suggests that changes in style have occurred.

Since the question of changes in home style among congressmen and senators has received little scholarly attention, most of the evidence to support this proposition is derived from studies with different objectives. Therefore, the findings may sometimes appear to be tangential to the question addressed in this analysis, but they do suggest the same conclusion—that there have been changes in home style.

One such piece of evidence is the observed change in the images and responsibilities of congressmen and senators. For instance, Herbert Asher's interviews with House incumbents reveal a shift in the amount of attention that congressmen devote to constituency services.

Constituency casework is heavier than ever before and the expansion of the federal government in the 1960's into such areas as education, poverty, medicare, and space has made the congressman an even more important link between constituency and government, particularly the national bureaucracy. A recurrent theme throughout the interviews was that the congressman had become an ombudsman. Many representatives either complained about or merely cited the heavier workload; they said they had more constituents with more problems and greater expectations. (Asher, 1975, p. 229)

The same observation has been made regarding the behavior of senators.

> Today's Senators must run errands for growing numbers of constituents, greet visitors, be seen at social functions, tend to committee work, berate bureaucrats, investigate, approve reports, placate friends, and, alas, a number must accept far-off speaking engagements for pay to balance the family budget. The typical Senator also must dig hard into the pork barrel on behalf of constituents for contracts, projects, loans. (Landauer, 1963, p. 16)

In short, congressmen and senators both appear to have altered their home styles in ways that emphasize their attention to constituency affairs; clearly, the differences between the two jobs are disappearing.

In Figure 1, I present data describing the mean number of days that congressmen and senators spent in their constituencies between 1958 and 1980. It is obvious from this graph that there have been significant increases. In later chapters I will examine these trends extensively. For now, it is only necessary to point out that the increases in the time spent in the constituency by congressmen and senators appear to coincide. That is, the trends in the amount of time that senators and representatives spend in their constituencies begin an upward movement during the middle of the 1960s and follow a monotonic course after that period. The major difference in the trends between district and state attentiveness is that congressmen appear to spend more time in their constituencies than senators.

What is particularly unusual about these trends is that they occur at the same time that institutional demands on congressmen and senators were also expanding (Figs. 2 and 3). Incumbents were being pulled in two directions during these years: legislative demands were absorbing more of their energies at the same time that constituency affairs were consuming more and more of their time. As Figures 2 and 3 illustrate, congressmen and senators were spending more time in voting (Fig. 2) and in session (Fig. 3) than in the past; they were also spending more time in their constituencies during the same period of time. While these activities seem to be zero-sum in terms of their demands on the time and energies of incumbents, Congress has developed ways of reducing these conflicting demands, such as structuring the legislative schedule to facilitate district and state attention. (For an extended discussion of this point, see chap. 4.)

Figure 1.
Time Spent in the Constituency by House and Senate Incumbents: 1959–1980

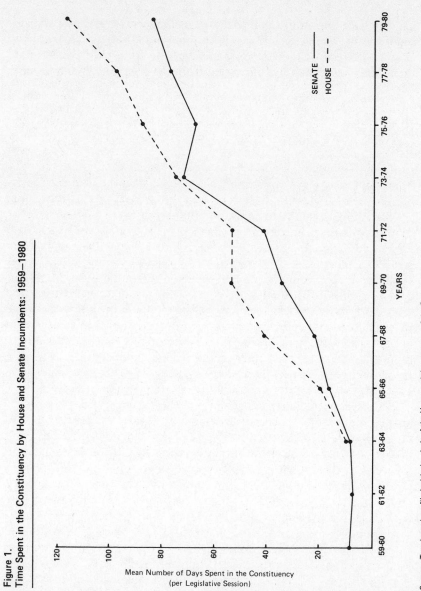

Mean Number of Days Spent in the Constituency
(per Legislative Session)

SENATE ———
HOUSE — — —

YEARS

Source: Travel vouchers filed with the clerk of the House and the secretary of the Senate.

Another important manifestation of this change in home style is the increase in casework loads. John Johannes (1980, p. 520) reports that 71 percent of the 193 staff members he surveyed believed that their office caseloads had increased from the past. Senators and rep-

Figure 2.
Recorded Votes per Congress by Representatives and Senators: 1947—1980

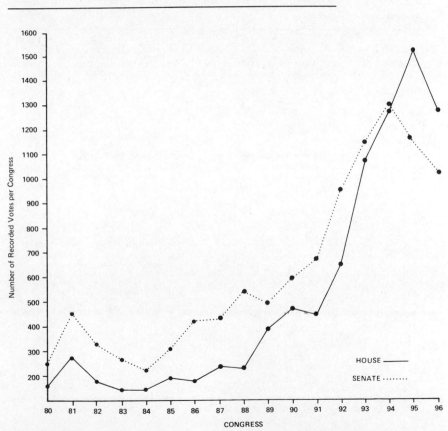

Source: Ornstein et al., 1982, pp. 130—33.

resentatives attribute this growth to the increase in government programs and bureaucratic procedures, but their staffs tend to feel that the members themselves are the causes of the increases (ibid., p. 521). The evidence suggests that incumbents may indeed be responsible. Certainly, they are making greater use of existing devices for maintaining contact with their constituents and stimulating their needs (ibid., Table 3, p. 523), and these efforts have actually increased casework loads (Johannes and McAdams, 1984). For example, many senators have initiated outreach programs to solicit complaints of constituents.

Even with project workers stationed in Washington, most offices are making increased efforts for outreach programs, both with groups and individuals in the States. These outreach programs range from traveling field representa-

Figure 3.
Days Spent in Session by Representatives and Senators (by Congress): 1947–1980

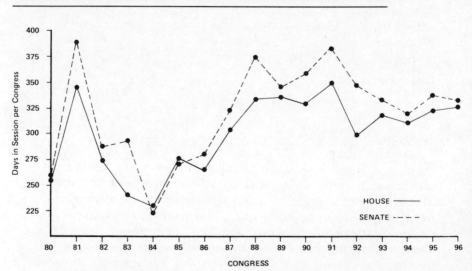

Source: Ornstein et al., 1982, pp. 130–33.

tives going from town to town, setting up a temporary office in community centers to listen to citizen opinions and complaints, to mobile van units which perform the same functions using the van as a mobile office. (Breslin, 1977, p. 25)

Another example of the increased attention that has been given to casework for constituents is that more legislative staff is being allocated by members to their district offices—the main center for dealing with the problems of the constituency. In 1972, congressmen allocated about 23 percent of their staff to their district offices, and senators about 13 percent to their state offices; by 1981 the number of congressional staff allocated to district offices increased to 36 percent, while the size of the senate staff located in the state doubled to 26 percent (Ornstein et al., 1982, p. 112). Similarly, Steven Schiff and Steven Smith (1983) report that the mean number of staff located in district offices doubled between 1968 (2.1 staff members) and 1976 (4.5 staff members). Morris Fiorina (1977, p. 58) makes the same point: the percentage of staff assigned to district offices increased between 1960 (14 percent) and 1974 (34 percent), and there also has been an increase in the number of multiple district offices. In sum, there is evidence of a change in the home styles of congressmen and senators; a basic element of this change is an increased attention to constituency affairs.

FACTORS PRECIPITATING CHANGE

Needs of Incumbents

Another theme in this study is that Congress has facilitated changes in home style among incumbents as it has attempted to accommodate their needs. There are at least three needs that appear to underlie the changes in style that I uncover: electoral security, freedom to pursue legislative goals, and service to constituents. As Congress attempted to satisfy members' demands in these three areas, it facilitated home-style changes by reducing the costs (to the members) associated with them. In this way, Congress has provided institutional incentives for members to adopt more attentive home styles.

Electoral Security

Electoral safety is a primary concern for many members of Congress; some might even say that it is the sole goal for most of them. While few political scientists have been able to uncover the effects of electoral security by using objective measures of electoral safety, there is a widespread belief among congressional scholars that electoral security is, nonetheless, important to every member of Congress. Certainly, objective measures may never quite match an incumbent's subjective impressions. To the congressional scholar, an incumbent who receives over 60 percent of the two-party vote is fairly safe, but incumbents may not reach the same conclusion about their own vulnerability. In short, electoral safety is a perspective on political life that varies according to "where you sit." Incumbents never appear to feel that they are as safe as more objective evaluations of their margins might suggest; hence electoral safety may be more important to the behavior of incumbents than current research indicates.

The electoral incentive appears to be a motivation for a variety of legislative activities. Mayhew, for example, views the desire for electoral safety as the motivating force behind a whole range of incumbent behaviors. "The electoral goal has an attractive universality to it. It has to be the *proximate* goal of everyone, the goal that must be achieved over and over if other ends are to be entertained" (Mayhew, 1974a, p. 16). According to Morris Fiorina, the electoral incentive serves as an impetus for the growth of federal programs, especially those that distribute particularistic benefits.

The bureaucracy serves as a convenient lightning rod for public frustration and a convenient whipping boy for congressmen. But so long as the bureaucracy accommodates congressmen, the latter will oblige with even larger budgets and grants of authority. Congress does not just react to big government—it creates it. All of Washington prospers. More and more bureaucrats promulgate more and more regulations and dispense more and more money. Fewer and fewer congressmen suffer electoral defeat. (Fiorina, 1977, p. 49)

Policy and Career Freedom

While electoral safety may be a basic goal for all members, in many cases it is only a means to an end, rather than an end in itself. Electoral safety is a precondition for assignment to many important and powerful legislative committees (Masters, 1961, p. 353) and appears to be a major consideration in the selection of party leaders (Peabody, 1976). Clearly, it furthers the attainment of other goals. In order to attain such goals, members must achieve some measure of freedom from their constituents; frequently, the size of a reelection margin is a good indicator of the level of freedom that an incumbent can expect to exercise in Washington. For instance, leadership positions normally require individuals to devote a considerable proportion of their time and energies to overseeing the operations of their congressional parties. Members with designs on leadership positions must demonstrate that they have sufficient freedom from their constituents to concentrate their energies on legislative business rather than constituency affairs; large reelection margins might be construed as evidence of an incumbent's level of freedom. Similarly, those who seek to develop national reputations as spokespersons for specific causes require some latitude to pursue and espouse controversial issues. Thus the attainment of positions of power and visibility are legislative goals that may require members to gain a level of freedom from constituents without fear of electoral reprisals.

Members may be able to "purchase" their freedom to pursue personal goals by demonstrating their concern for the welfare of their districts or states. Incumbents compensate their constituents for the latitude granted by being attentive to district and state affairs. The case that incumbents want to make is that the pursuit of other legislative goals will not interfere with, disrupt, or alter their attention to constituency affairs. Changes toward greater attention to the district or state seem likely to alleviate the concern of constituents that their congressman or senator has lost interest in constituency affairs.

Service to Constituents

The final factor that has precipitated the change in home style is the growth in the demands of constituents during recent decades. The explosion in federal programs during the 1960s sparked an increase in demands, needs, and expectations on the part of constituents. Casework demands on senators and congressmen have increased dramatically, and there has been a corresponding increase in the number of citizens who have written to their congressman since the 1960s (Fig. 4).[1] In short, citizens are more dependent upon their congressmen and senators than in the past, as is demonstrated by the increases in the casework loads of incumbents and the rise in contact that constituents have with their legislators. As a result, there have been changes in the institution and in the behavior of members that are aimed at sustaining congressional responsiveness.

While these goals have probably existed collectively and individually for decades, they assumed unusual importance in the 1960s and 1970s. As Fiorina (1977) has suggested, constituents' demands reached an unusual level as a result of the explosion of federal programs during the 1960s. Electoral safety has been a concern for some time, but it, too, reached a critical level in the 1960s as large numbers of new senators and congressmen were elected from areas that were politically atypical of their own partisan and ideological identi-

Figure 4.
Trends in the Percentage of the Electorate Writing to Their Member of Congress, 1947–1976

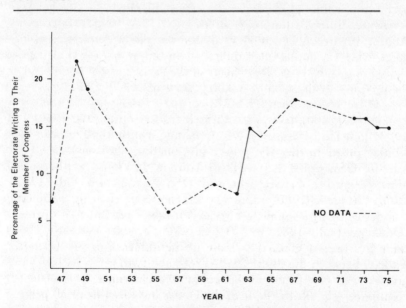

Sources: American Institute for Public Opinion, and Center for Political Studies, 1964 and 1968.

fications. The goal of preserving freedom in Washington may also have gained support since the 1960s because of the increased dividends that such leeway could pay in terms of other legislative goals such as power and influence.

Expansion of Institutional Opportunities

The expansion in the opportunities for members to exercise congressional influence during this period may have been an important motivation for efforts to enhance their freedom from their constituents. For example, the increased use of unanimous consent agreements for organizing Senate business during the 1960s and 1970s (Oleszek, 1978, p. 144) gave individual senators a greater voice in determining the schedule; this also served to increase their involvement in Senate decision making. Further, the decision in the 1950s by the Senate minority leader, Lyndon Johnson, to guarantee every Democratic senator a choice committee assignment provided greater access to positions of power for junior members—a change from Senate traditions. "Johnson's decision in 1953 to guarantee every senator, regardless of seniority, at least one major committee assignment reflected, among other things, a conviction that the choice spots should be available to all members of the party and not remain solely the province of the senior senators" (Stewart, 1971, p. 65).

In the House, there is evidence that Democratic liberals were gaining bargaining leverage with their leaders during the 1960s and 1970s (Sinclair, 1983) and were pursuing institutional reforms that would spread further the power in Congress (Ornstein, 1975). At least for Democrats, the power structure in the House was becoming more permeable: between the 84th (1955–1956) and 90th (1967–1968) Congresses, the proportion of Democrats chairing a standing committee or subcommittee increased from 27 percent to 45 percent (Ornstein et al., 1982, p. 101). In addition, since the early 1960s there has been a gradual increase in the influence of subcommittee leaders: between the 86th (1959–1960) and 95th (1977–1978) Congresses, the proportion of subcommittee chairmen who managed committee bills on the floor of the House increased from 30 percent to 67 percent (Smith and Deering, 1984, p. 195). This represents a significant shift in power since floor managers direct the course of debate and play a central role in guiding bills through the House.

They plan strategy and parliamentary maneuvers to meet changing floor situations; they respond to points of order; they protect bills from weakening amendments (in the case of the majority), or promote such amendments (in the case of the minority); they alert supporters to be on the floor to vote for or against certain amendments; they advise colleagues on the meaning and importance of amendments; they judge when committee amendments should be offered or deferred; they inform party leaders of member sentiment and the mood of the House toward the bill; they control the time for general debate and can act to limit debate on amendments, sections or titles of the bill, or the entire measure. (Oleszek, 1978, p. 112)

The increase in the number of subcommittee chairmen exercising this influence is indicative of the greater opportunities for House members to participate in a meaningful way in the policy process. This is especially important because committee chairmen have normally reserved this position of power for themselves. Thus the greater permeability of the power structures in Congress (e.g., committees and subcommittees)[2] created incentives for incumbents to maximize their freedom from the opinions of constituents; such freedom could permit them some leeway from interference by constituents in their personal pursuit and exercise of power in Congress. This may account for the emphasis that incumbents place on explaining their pursuit of power to their constituents (Fenno, 1978).

One expression of the desire to maintain freedom in Washington is the growth in the percentage of congressmen who envision their legislative role as that of the trustee as opposed to the delegate. The trustee role gives greater latitude to the individual representative in making legislative decisions; the delegate role constrains decisions by requiring them to coincide with district opinion. Simply put, trustees view their legislative responsibilities as requiring them to exercise their best judgment on the legislative matters before them; delegates, in contrast, take their cues on policy matters from their constituents rather than the dictates of their own conscience. While the data presented in Table 1 are not directly comparable since the categorization of roles was based on different types of questions, the pattern suggests that a significant change has occurred in the way House incumbents view their legislative responsibilities. The number of congressmen who would follow their conscience rather than district opinion, when a conflict between the two occurs, has increased be-

Table 1
Style of Representation Among the Mass Public and House Members

Style of Representation	Mass Public		House Members	
	1968[a]	1977[b]	1958[c]	1977[d]
Follow conscience	30%	22%	51%	65%
Follow district	43	46	7	5
Depends on issue	23	27	38	25
Not sure	4	5	5	3
N	1,534	1,531	158	142

a. "When there is a conflict between what a U.S. representative feels is best and what the people in his district want, do you think he should follow his own conscience or follow what the people in the district want?"

b. "When there is a conflict between what your congressman feels is best and what he thinks the people in the district want, do you think he should follow his own conscience or follow what the people in the district want?"

c. 1958 question: "As a member of Congress, if you want to take a particular stand on a bill that is before the House, but feel that a majority of the people in your district would want you to take a different stand, what would you probably do?" (Center for Political Studies, 1958 American Representation Study).

d. 1977 question: "When there is a conflict between what you feel is best and what you think the people in your district want, do you think you should follow your own conscience or follow what the people in your district want?" (U.S. Congress, 1977).

tween 1958 and 1977. At the same time, mass opinion continues to indicate that district opinion should *always* be followed (Table 1).

Further, congressmen may be placing a greater emphasis on responding to national rather than local needs (Table 2). This shift in orientations suggests that a movement toward greater freedom from constituents has occurred among House incumbents. A bare majority of the House members surveyed in 1958 preferred a style of representation that provided only a modicum of freedom from their constituents (Table 1). By 1977, the proportion of House incumbents that desired greater freedom from district opinion had increased to 65 percent.

At the same time as the trustee orientation was rising, services to

Table 2
Focus of Representation Among Congressmen

Focus of Representation	1963[a]	1977[b]
Nation dominant	28%	45%
Nation and district equal	23	28
District dominant	42	24
Unclassified	8	3
N	87	145

a. 1963 responses determined from open-ended interviews with House incumbents (Davidson, 1969, p. 122).
b. "Do you feel that you should be primarily concerned with looking after the needs and interests of your own district, or do you feel that you should be primarily concerned with looking after the needs and interests of the nation as a whole?" (U.S. Congress, 1977, p. 887).

the constituency were gaining broader approval among congressmen. For instance, in 1958 only about two of every five congressional candidates interviewed felt that these were a "very important" job responsibility. By 1977 more than one-half of the incumbents interviewed (in a separate study) believed that getting back to the district, helping people with governmental problems, and explaining the actions of government, were "very important" constituency activities (Table 3). In short, the differing levels of support for services to the constituency in 1958 and 1977 suggest that a pronounced change has occcured in the home styles of congressmen.

Services to the constituency are more important than in the past, but the motivations to maintain political individuality have also grown in strength. These trends are not as inconsistent as they might seem. In fact, they may be causally linked. By behaving like delegates in terms of their attentiveness to district affairs, trustees create levels of constituent trust comparable to that created by the representational styles of delegates. This enables trustees to exercise a measure of freedom in their policy behaviors.

In sum, the needs of incumbents for electoral security, greater freedom in Washington, and service to constituents, together with

Table 3
Importance of Constituency Service to Congressmen

	%
1958[a] Importance of constituency service	39
1977[b] Getting back to district to stay in touch with constituents	74
Helping people in the district who have personal problems with the government	58
Taking the time to explain to citizens what their government is doing to solve important problems and why	53

a. Figures drawn from Center for Political Studies, 1958 American Representation Study, p. 77.
b. Figures drawn from U.S. Congress, 1977, pp. 879–82.

the expansion of institutional opportunities, have fueled the changes in home style that I describe in the following chapters. These conditions fostered the growth of perquisites that facilitated changes in home style during this period.

INCENTIVES FOR CHANGE

Some changes in the attention that congressmen and senators devote to their constituencies can be explained by changes in the goals of individual members. Subsets of legislators may alter their home styles in response to the same set of conditions, but individual changes normally do not effect all members. Aggregate change, on the other hand, occurs as large segments of Congress systematically shift their attention to their constituencies in response to institutional or societal conditions.

Individual Change

There are at least three major causes of individual changes in home style: strategic, personal, and contextual (Fenno, 1978, p. 195). Fenno suggests that a strategic cause for incumbents to intensify their levels of attentiveness to their constituency could occur with declines in electoral support in primary or general elections. There are two personal causes that, according to Fenno, are linked to shifts in the goals of incumbents. Congressmen seeking to run for higher office frequently intensify their contact with their constituents in order to expand their base of electoral support. In this case, change in style is driven by the ambition of the member. On the other hand, incumbents who are planning to retire can be expected to rid themselves of demands by their constituents by reducing their levels of contact and cultivation: changes in home style under these conditions result from the disappearance of the electoral incentive. Finally, Fenno suggests that contextual change, that is, change in the nature of the congressional district brought about by population or geographical changes, can induce changes in the attentiveness with which incumbents treat their constituents. Any time incumbents experience conditions that necessitate the rebuilding of electoral support, such as redistricting, the contextual change may produce a change in the individual attentiveness of members. I examine these hypotheses in the next chapter.

Aggregate Change

Aggregate changes in attention result from three processes: seniority, cohort, and period effects. Congressional careers can be viewed as proceeding through various sequences. For example, Larry Dodd (1977) suggests that the goals of members shift over time as incumbents gain seniority and electoral safety. We can also visualize a career cycle associated with attention to the constituency: new senators and congressmen might be attentive to their districts and states at first, but as they attain positions of congressional influence, their interest shifts from constituency affairs to national and ideological issues. Thus seniority effects suggest a "political life cycle" (Matthews, 1973) that predicts declining attentiveness with seniority: the increases in attention that do transpire are only temporary and produced by initial states of electoral insecurity. Aggregate changes in attentiveness could also result from the general replacement of older cohorts of less attentive legislators by generations of more attentive ones—the cohort effect. As these generational dynamics proceed, aggregate levels of attentiveness are increased. These generational changes can result from differences in recruitment processes (Payne, 1980) or conditions at the time of entry into Congress (Fiorina, 1977). Finally, period effects are reflected in changes in attention associated with specific periods of time. In this study, period effects are associated with increases in the perquisites of office. These "perks" have motivated members to convert to higher levels of state or district attentiveness. For example, increases in office allowances serve as incentives for incumbents to devote greater resources to the cultivation of their constituents. Period effects are often exhibited in the conversion of all members to higher levels of district or state attention. In sum, aggregate changes in attentiveness to constituency can theoretically be brought about by seniority, cohort, and period effects; in chapter 3, I examine the degree to which these effects have fostered shifts in the attentiveness of congressmen and senators during recent decades.

THE FACILITATION OF CHANGE BY CONGRESS

Congress facilitated changes in style among congressmen and senators as it accommodated their needs. While there are a variety of ways in which Congress can directly or indirectly facilitate these changes, increasing the perquisites of office and structuring the congressional schedule to foster legislator-constituent contact are perhaps two of the most explicit. These helped to shape the opportunity structure in Congress by subsidizing resources for establishing contacts with constituents and by reducing the conflict between legislative (Washington) responsibilities and those to constituents. In these ways Congress reduced the "costs" of attention to the constituency and facilitated increased attentiveness.

Increases in Perquisites
David Mayhew (1974a) and others (Cover, 1977; Fiorina, 1977; Parker, 1980b) have called attention to the growth in the perquisites

available to congressmen and senators. In addition to the growth in salary, other emoluments of the job have undergone parallel increases. Personal and committee staffs and various congressional allowances, such as those for telephone and travel, have grown considerably. These perquisites enable members to satisfy a number of goals. Staff, for example, can shoulder some of the burden of contact with constituents. For many constituents, a staff member or caseworker is the only contact that they will have with the congressional office. In fact, staff are expected to shield their bosses from constituents' complaints and to execute their responsibilities to the constituency with a minimum of involvement on the part of the senator or congressman. The less involved a member is in the services to the constituency, the more time that can be devoted to other matters that do require personal attention.

In most instances, casework and services to constituents do not suffer when placed in the hands of the office staff. While direct communication with a senator or congressman may prompt a quicker response from an agency, staff members frequently invoke their member's name in correspondence with agencies and, therefore, achieve the same end. Clearly, bureaucrats realize that some of what crosses their desks is of relatively minor concern to a legislator. But since they have difficulty in differentiating between what is important and what the staff says is important to their boss, bureaucrats respond in the same fashion to all routine congressional inquiries. Some staff members may actually be more effective than their members in their interactions with the federal bureaucracy because they, not their bosses, have developed contacts within specific agencies. Office staff and committee staff also provide essential legislative services by acting as conduits for information from groups and agency officials. Such assistance frees members to pursue other objectives without letting legislative responsibilities or those to the constituency slip. In short, Congress has made service to the district less costly by increasing the staff resources available to incumbents. Perhaps the best example of this effect is the decision in the House to authorize members to hire an additional staff member for the sole purpose of handling communications with constituents.

In addition to increases in staff, other perquisites of office have been steadily increased. New allowances have been established, and existing ones have increased their base. House travel allowances, for example, experienced an enormous increase from 2 subsidized trips per year in 1963 to a maximum of 32 per year in 1979. The increase in these perquisites provided incentives for members to exploit these resources more fully, especially since failure to do so would result in forfeiting the funds (all unspent funds are automatically returned to the Treasury). Like the proverbial tail-wagging-the-dog analogy, increases in such perquisites may have stimulated greater attention to the constituency. I will say more about the increases in incumbent perquisites and their impact on attentiveness in chapter 4.

Adjustment of the Congressional Schedule

The conflict between responsibilities in Washington and in the constituency is resolved for incumbents by structuring the legislative agenda to permit both. That is, the legislative schedule is partitioned into periods for contact with the constituency (district work periods, recesses) and congressional business. The Tuesday-to-Thursday schedule of legislative business in the House is one example of how legislative schedules can be organized to satisfy members' needs for contact with the constituency: "Indeed, most floor action in Congress takes place on Tuesday, Wednesday and Thursday to accommodate members' home visits" ("For Many Incumbents," 1979, p. 1354). The New York congressional delegation has found such a schedule especially useful in satisfying expectations on the part of constituents of frequent personal contact with their representatives (Fiellin, 1962).

In the Senate, it is essential to arrange the agenda of business to accommodate the needs of members because it is normally organized under unanimous consent agreements. This means that the legislative schedule must be appropriate to everyone. This is not really a problem since most Senate leaders are willing to alter business to accommodate the schedules of others (Oleszek, 1978). Usually, leader-follower consultation precedes the development of such unanimous consent motions, so that members do not find it necessary to object to the legislative schedules fashioned by their leaders.[3] Since bipartisan consultation occurs among Senate leaders, no partisan advantages are gained from the organization of Senate business.

Thus the perquisites of office have provided incentives for members to alter their existing styles of attention to the constituency, and the legislative schedule has been organized to minimize conflicts between congressional business and contact with the constituency. In these ways Congress has reduced the costs of tending to the constituency and facilitated changes in home style on the part of congressmen and senators.

CONCLUSIONS

I have now defined the general contours of the analysis that follows and the questions that I will address. There are three major themes. First, that a change has occurred in home style, a change that has placed a greater emphasis on attention to constituency affairs. Second, that this change has been facilitated by Congress as it has accommodated the needs of its members by increasing various perquisites and by structuring the legislative schedule. Finally, that these changes have been accompanied by changes in the electoral safety of incumbent congressmen and senators that have reduced House and Senate turnover and altered the operations of Congress.

: 2 :

Individual Changes
in Home Style

THE TENDENCY TOWARD STABILITY

While this analysis is devoted to change in home styles, no discussion of such change would be complete without noting the stability of styles. A major attribute of home styles is their permanence; once established, the patterns that mark them tend to persist. This is not to say that home styles are immutable. It would be more accurate to say that they are susceptible to change, but only when there are sufficient incentives. In most cases, the forces of stability preclude significant changes. This stability can be explained by four factors: the strategies adopted by incumbents, the expectations of constituents, the natural course of congressional careers, and the absence of incentives.

Most incumbents want their constituents to see patterns in their home-style activities that reinforce the images they are constantly "polishing" and promulgating in their personal visits with constituents and in their communications within the district or state. As well as engendering political support at home, home styles are designed to mesh with the personalities and goals of congressmen and senators. Given this, a successful home style represents the fit between personal goals and the electoral necessities that confront a member. This congruence tends to promote the maintenance of the existing pattern of behavior; this is especially true since most incumbents probably have no clear idea of what aspects of their home style are responsible for what proportion of their electoral support (Fenno, 1978). Such uncertainty motivates members to continue existing patterns of behavior. The simple strategy under these conditions would be to do the same things in the future that proved so successful in the past. As Fenno notes (ibid., p. 125), it is prudent for congressmen to "do just what we did last time."

In creating an image, an incumbent may also be limiting the capacity to change that home style in the future. Members mold the expectations of constituents as they establish their home styles. These expectations, in turn, constrain that home style because members feel that their constituents expect certain behaviors and would react negatively to any attempt to alter them. "If these House members failed to see ten people in Maple Grove or cancelled the open meetings or relinquished caucus leadership or left immediately after the clambake, they believe it would cost them dearly in electoral support. They might lose support they had "last time," because they believe that their present home style helped them to victory last time" (ibid., p. 191).

Home styles also harden over the course of legislative careers. Fenno identifies two stages in the careers of incumbents: an expansionist stage and a protectionist stage. Incumbents in the expansionist stage seek to expand the bounds of their existing electoral coalition and to solidify a core of strong support. During the protectionist stage, in contrast, they become less interested in building support and more concerned about maintaining the electoral support they have already attained. Home-style activities in the protectionist stage can be described as preventive maintenance. As careers move from the expansionist to the protectionist stage, home styles harden. "The expansionist stage during which the congressman cultivates first a primary constituency, then a reelection constituency and during which he works out a viable, comfortable home style, has a largely experimental impulse to it. Once in the protectionist stage, however, the dominant impulse is conservative" (ibid., p. 189).

Finally, home styles may be resistant to change because there are just too few incentives to alter an already successful style. Home styles represent the culmination of political experiences and experimentations: an optimal, and carefully constructed, fit between personal goals and aspirations on the one hand and the image and behavior cultivated in the constituency on the other. Changes in these patterned behaviors, therefore, require strong incentives. The pressures for stability seem likely to counter most incentives for altering home styles. Only incentives that can satisfy for the member a variety of needs, perhaps simultaneously, seem capable of inducing widespread changes in style.

HOW AND WHY HOME STYLES CHANGE

Changes in home style reflect modifications in presentation of self, in explanation of Washington activity, and in allocation of resources to the constituency. For example, incumbents can alter their presentations—the images they project to their constituents. An extremely close election, for instance, led one of Fenno's congressmen to alter his issue-oriented image and style. "Through the 1968 campaign, I played the role of teacher and preacher, persuading people of what I thought was right . . . I went to lots of political meetings. When I almost lost, we realized that this was not going to be a successful way of campaigning. I decided then to shake hands as much as I could" (ibid., p. 197).

Congressmen and senators can also alter their explanations. One way of doing this is in terms of the application of a delegate or trustee rationale for explaining Washington behavior (especially voting behavior) to constituents. "If, when they are deciding how to vote, House members think in terms of delegates and trustees, it is because they are thinking about the terms in which they will explain (i.e., justify or legitimate) that vote back home if the need to do so arises" (ibid., p. 161). Members may explain and legitimate their votes by justifying them as the expression of the opinion of constituents (delegate), or as the exercise of the incumbent's best judgment (trustee). One factor that might promote a change in the way members explain their activity is electoral safety. As members gain electoral safety, one might expect them to be more willing to express and follow opinions that deviate from those held by a majority of their constituents. Roger Davidson (1969, pp. 127–29) has demonstrated a relationship between the delegate-trustee dichotomy and electoral marginality: delegate roles are more frequently selected by representatives from competitive districts, while trustees are more apt to represent safe districts than marginal ones.

Incumbents also can change the resources they devote to constituency affairs. An explicit expression of changes in the allocation of resources would be the adoption of more attentive home styles. Incumbents, for example, might increase the number of newsletters sent to constituents, or the amount of time spent in the state or district.

If one wants to decribe changes in home styles, it is necessary to consider the whole constellation of behaviors that involve presentation, explanation, and allocation of resources to the constituency. Unfortunately, it is virtually impossible to gain a diachronic perspective on how members have changed their presentations or explanations. Since the identification and study of home-style behaviors is a relatively recent phenomenon, sparked by Fenno's study of the House (1978), there is no historical record that might provide a baseline for observing changes in these behaviors. And it is unlikely that such historical information could be retrieved by asking current members to recall past home-style behaviors or how these have changed over time. This method is apt to produce information that is susceptible to distortion since the accuracy of recalled behavior is always suspect. Further, the problems inherent in trying to monitor the home styles of congressmen and senators are difficult, if not impossible, to surmount. Fenno's "Notes on Method" in *Home Style* (1978, pp. 249–95) is an account of the significant personal costs involved in conducting the type of participant observation that could provide useful longitudinal information. Fenno's unusual dedication made *Home Style* possible, but the sacrifices required and the personal costs involved seem certain to discourage others from following the same research strategy.

One can obtain information, however, on patterns in resource allocations over time because of the extensive public records that have been maintained regarding the allocations of office resources. This means that one can identify changes in how members allocate staff and personal time to constituency affairs. While the changes in such resource allocations provide a continuous, longitudinal record of modifications in one element of the home style of incumbents, they cannot provide a complete picture of how styles have changed.

PERSONAL TIME AS A MEASURE OF CHANGE

A concern with changes over time forces reliance upon information regarding changes in resource allocations as a basis for inferences about changes in style. I realize that this is only a partial view, but I feel that the changes that I describe—increased displays of attentiveness—permeate other home-style behaviors, such as the presentation of self and the explanation of Washington activity. Changes in patterns of resource allocation and usage therefore can be used as indicators of changes in attentiveness. If House and Senate incumbents increase the resources devoted to constituency affairs, the increased attentiveness can be viewed as representing a change: the adoption of an attentive home style. An attentive home style is a image that reinforces, and is reinforced by, home-style activities. For instance, attentive incumbents might emphasize their accessibility to constituents and service to the district in there personal contacts with constituents, or stress their helpfulness in other presentations in the constituency. Explanations of Washington activity might emphasize constituent-related benefits, such as federal projects or monies diverted to the district or state, in justifying votes or legislative actions. For this reason, I speak of changes in attention to the constituency as if they penetrated every aspect of a member's home style, although the empirical basis for my generalizations is restricted to patterns in resource allocations over time.

The attentiveness of senators to their states symbolizes their concern for the state and its constituents in the same way that such attention convinces voters that the House member is looking after the congressional district (Parker, 1980a). As Donald Matthews has observed, "a senator's well-publicized presence in the home state symbolizes that he has not forgotten the people who put him in power." Senators, like House incumbents, also find that the allocation of personal time to constituency visits conflicts "with the proper performance of legislative responsibilities" (Matthews, 1973, p. 229). This conflict is vividly displayed in Figures 2 and 3 (chap. 1), which represent the amount of time that senators and representatives have devoted to their legislative duties.

I have measured the attentiveness of incumbents in terms of the number of days that they spent in their states or districts while the Senate or House was in session. These data are coded from the travel vouchers filed with the secretary of the Senate and the clerk of the House. While there are a variety of measures that can serve as useful indicators of attentiveness, the time spent in the district or state has a number of distinct advantages.

Perhaps the most important advantage is that time spent in the constituency may be a better measure of change in home style than measures of other perquisite usage (mass mailings, staff, district offices) because it is more sensitive to shifts in the priorities and goals of individual members. Unlike other congressional resources, it reflects a personal investment of incumbents' time in the affairs of their districts and states that cannot be easily transferred to others. While a portion of the burden can be shifted to staff, the jobs of image building and explaining are tasks that each senator and congressman must do personally. This is not to deny that staff members frequently travel to the constituency at the request of their bosses, but such attention is usually rendered as a supplement to that of the congressman or senator. However, it rarely compensates for the lack of a member's *personal* attention. Incumbents can shift some of the costs of attention to their staffs, who can perform constituency duties adequately and effectively. Thus some constituency activities may not be very sensitive to the types of change in attention that have occurred, because incumbents have not had to incur the costs entirely on their own. "Members of Congress, themselves, spend little time on case and project work. . . . Rather, they have increased steadily the sizes of their casework staffs and moved them to offices in their home districts" (Johannes, 1981, p. 80).

Time spent in the state or district, on the other hand, entails personal costs to the member that are not easily transferred to someone else. As Donald Matthews (1973, p. 229) noted with respect to senators, "while at home, it is hard for a senator to insulate himself from constituent demands on his time and attention." Time spent in the constituency is a nontransferrable cost for incumbents. They have to meet with their constituents; they cannot avoid the face-to-face interactions that they are normally sheltered from in Washington. Clearly, time spent in the state or district imposes burdens on members that may be as demanding as their legislative responsibilities. Some have argued that these activities are even more demanding.

There are three reasons why time spent in the state or district would be sensitive to the types of changes in home style that I seek to uncover. First, incumbents cannot insulate themselves from the demands of constituents while at home, and such demands are rather onerous. Therefore, time spent in the state or district is not taken lightly by incumbents. It is hard work. Second, time spent in the constituency conflicts with legislative responsibilities (ibid., p. 220; Fenno, 1978, p. 34) and hence represents the allocation of a scarce resource—the personal time and energies of the incumbent. Finally, such attention entails costs that are borne entirely by the incumbent since there is little chance of transferring them to someone else. Despite these drawbacks, attention to the constituency is critical because it provides opportunities for congressmen and senators to reinforce that often repeated message, "I care about you and I am looking after your interests."

Another advantage of using time spent in the constituency to measure attentiveness is that one can obtain a reliable and unobtrusive measure of the amount of time that incumbents spend without having to rely upon information from more reactive sources such as staff or member estimates.[1] The measure also appears to be free of a number of biases that might confound the analysis. One potential source of distortion in the measurement of the attentiveness of senators is that "the farther senators live from Washington, the more difficult it is for them to get home" (Fenno, 1982, p. 34). That is, there may exist an inherent "distance bias." Measuring attentiveness in terms of the number of days spent in the district or state, rather than the number of trips, should reduce the possibility of such a distortion. By using days spent, one allows for the fact that members who live farther away may spend more time when they do return home.

I have categorized the fifty states in terms of their distances from Washington, D.C. and, within each distance category, recorded the mean number of days spent in the state and district each Congress by senators and congressmen. These data are presented in Tables 4 and 5

Table 4
Distance from Washington and the Mean Number of Days Spent in the State
by Senators per Congress, 1959–1980[a]

	Distance from Washington in Miles					
	0–500	500–1000	1000–2000	Over 2000	eta^2	r^2
1959–1960	14.0 (22)[b]	11.5 (30)	16.5 (25)	24.9 (14)	.04	.02
1961–1962	8.0 (21)	15.4 (30)	17.6 (26)	16.5 (16)	.06	.04
1963–1964	10.1 (22)	16.0 (29)	20.3 (26)	28.3 (16)	.13	.13
1965–1966	32.0 (22)	32.3 (30)	33.6 (26)	49.9 (17)	.06	.04
1967–1968	37.4 (22)	34.3 (30)	46.5 (26)	56.6 (17)	.07	.06
1969–1970	53.1 (22)	64.0 (29)	76.7 (26)	91.5 (17)	.10	.10
1971–1972	94.2 (21)	73.4 (30)	73.7 (26)	98.3 (17)	.04	.00
1973–1974	139.3 (21)	121.6 (30)	162.7 (26)	159.9 (16)	.05	.02
1975–1976	135.7 (22)	134.0 (30)	147.2 (26)	136.2 (16)	.01	.00
1977–1978	184.9 (22)	154.7 (29)	148.0 (24)	123.9 (16)	.03	.03
1979–1980	177.0 (22)	183.1 (30)	163.0 (26)	137.0 (16)	.04	.03

Source: Travel vouchers of U.S. senators, 1959–1980.
a. Distance is *not* statistically significant at the .001 level at any time period.
b. Number of senators in that category.

and they support my contention that there is no distance bias when time
spent is used as a measure of attentiveness. Among senators, there is
only one Congress (1963–1964) in which a strong relationship (alpha
< .01) exists between distance and the time spent in the state, and in this

Table 5
Distance from Washington and the Mean Number of Days Spent in the
District by Congressmen per Congress, 1963–1980

| | Distance from Washington in Miles | | | | | | |
	0–500	500–1000	1000–1500	1500–2000	Over 2000	eta^2	r^2
1963–1964	11.5 (110)[a]	18.2 (130)	16.8 (53)	18.6 (10)	19.1 (51)	.04	.02
1965–1966	38.5 (58)	42.2 (137)	35.1 (54)	38.5 (11)	41.0 (53)	.01	.00
1967–1968	86.2 (40)	90.9 (127)	75.7 (56)	75.2 (11)	81.2 (55)	.05	.02
1969–1970	107.3 (34)	109.8 (128)	101.0 (58)	109.9 (10)	108.3 (56)	.01	.00
1971–1972	104.9 (46)	108.4 (134)	104.4 (54)	116.7 (11)	105.2 (58)	.01	.00
1973–1974	154.5 (60)	150.5 (133)	140.3 (55)	170.3 (12)	149.1 (62)	.03	.00
1975–1976[b]	193.3 (63)	182.3 (139)	171.4 (53)	194.0 (12)	147.0 (62)	.10	.08
1977–1978[b]	218.5 (134)	196.8 (140)	187.2 (57)	197.6 (12)	162.0 (63)	.05	.05
1979–1980	257.5 (135)	235.8 (141)	215.4 (57)	220.8 (12)	208.5 (62)	.04	.03

Source: Travel vouchers of U.S. congressmen, 1963–1980.
a. Number of congressmen in that category.
b. Statistically significant cross-sectional differences (ANOVA) at .001 level.

case, proximity to Washington is *not* associated with greater attentiveness. Excluding the last few years, senators from states farther from Washington appear to spend more time in their states than those who represented states closer to the capital; however, none of these relationships attains reasonable levels of significance.

The relationship between distance and time spent in the constituency is somewhat stronger among House incumbents than among senators. In the 94th (1975–1976) and 95th (1977–1978) Congresses, congressmen from districts close to the capital spent significantly more time in their districts than those from districts further from Washington (Table 5). At all other times, the relationship between distance and district attention is not highly significant. The infrequency of a statistical relationship suggests that no consistent distance bias exists in the measurement of district attention. Generally speaking, incumbents with districts or states closer to Capitol Hill spend more time in their constituencies than others, but few of these relationships are statistically significant.

Nor is there any evidence of a nonlinear relationship between distance from Washington and the mean number of days spent in the district or state. The last two columns of Tables 4 and 5 report two statistics: eta^2 and r^2. Eta^2 provides an estimation of the extent to which there is a significant nonlinear pattern in the relationship between distance and state attention. The r^2 statistic provides an estimation of the extent to which there is a linear pattern to the relationship between the two. A comparison between the magnitudes of the eta^2 and r^2 statistics provides an indication of the extent to which a nonlinear relationship can better account for variation between state attention and distance. For instance, in 1971–1972 senators close to (0–500 miles) and far from (over 2,000 miles) the capital spent more time in their states than those between 500 and 2,000 miles from Washington. The eta^2 statistic (.04) indicates that while a nonlinear relationship can explain more of the variation between distance from Washington and state attention than a linear relationship ($r^2 = .00$), the nonlinear pattern is no more statistically significant than the linear one.

As Tables 4 and 5 reveal, few of the nonlinear relationships represent a substantial improvement over the explanatory power of a linear relationship. The r^2 is generally equal in magnitude to the nonlinear measurement (eta^2), and both are generally insignificant. Hence there is no evidence to suggest that the relationship between distance from Washington and the attention devoted to state or district is significant either linearly or nonlinearly.

Despite their value in measuring attentiveness, the data derived from the travel vouchers may be subject to some distortion. That is, the absolute levels of attention may not be an accurate representation of the amount of time a senator or congressman actually spends in the state or district because travel may be subsidized by other sources and this time would not be reflected in the travel vouchers. For example, senators with large air force bases in their states probably receive occasional trips back home on military transport that would be directly subsidized by the Defense Department. As a result, the measure of attentiveness is probably conservative in that it may underestimate the actual amount of time spent in the state. The consequences of this measurement bias, however, are minimized by the emphasis placed on change in home style rather than on the absolute levels of district or state attention. Change in home style is measured by computing the difference in the amount of time congressmen and senators spend in consecutive terms of office:

$$\text{Stylistic Change} = \begin{bmatrix} \text{number of days spent} \\ \text{at time } t \\ \text{in district or state} \end{bmatrix} - \begin{bmatrix} \text{number of days spent} \\ \text{at time } t-1 \\ \text{in district or state} \end{bmatrix}$$

STABILITY IN ATTENTIVENESS

As with other elements of home style, there is considerable stability in the allocation of personal attention to the district or state. Tables 6 and 7 display the correlations between the number of days spent in the district or state in consecutive congresses. I have divided these data further according to cohort, or the time when the incumbent was first elected. These are collapsed into six-year periods to ensure an adequate number of cases for analysis.

An examination of the correlations within these cohorts reveals several interesting patterns. There is considerable stability in the patterns of attention to constituency among both congressmen and senators, although the latter appear to display somewhat greater stability (Table 6), a fact that is even more remarkable when one considers the six-year term of senators. The longer term permits them greater latitude than representatives in allocating their time to state affairs. With a six-year time span between elections, senators have greater flexibility in timing their visits to the state. One might expect them,

Table 6
Paired-Sample Correlations Between the Number of Days Spent in the State
During Consecutive Congresses

Years Correlated	Year Elected (Senate Cohort)				
	Before 1958	1958– 1963	1964– 1969	1970– 1975	1976– 1979
59–60/61–62	.22	.53			
61–62/63–64	.63[a]	.49			
63–64/65–66	.52[a]	.49[a]			
65–66/67–68	.40	.57[a]	.78		
67–68/69–70	.55[a]	.79[a]	.54		
69–70/71–72	.49	.86[a]	.33		
71–72/73–74	.67[a]	.59[a]	.62[a]	.63	
73–74/75–76	.77[a]	.74[a]	.61	.76[a]	
75–76/77–78	.76[a]	.81[a]	.83[a]	.30	
77–78/79–80	.46	.53	.77	.04	.77[a]

a. .001 level of significance.

therefore, to exhibit more irregular patterns of attention. For example, they might intensify their contacts with constituents in the years prior to the next election (Fenno, 1982). In fact, there is some evidence that senators do not give voters the same level of personal attention throughout the term (Taggert and Durant, 1984).

In the House, two patterns persist that are not as clearly evident in the Senate. First, there is some evidence that the allocations of personal time to the district gain stability with time (Table 7). This is illustrated by the increasing magnitude of the correlations between time spent in the district during successive Congresses. While senators also exhibit some increased stability in this respect, the pattern is not as clear as among congressmen. Second, older House incumbents appear to exhibit greater consistency in their attentiveness than younger cohorts. In most instances, the Congress-by-Congress correlations are larger among the more senior cohorts. The growing stabil-

Table 7
Paired-Sample Correlations Between the Number of Days Spent in the
District During Consecutive Congresses

Years Correlated	Year Elected (House Cohort)				
	Before 1958	1958– 1963	1964– 1969	1970– 1975	1976– 1979
63–64/65–66	.19	.18			
65–66/67–68	.35[a]	.19	.31		
67–68/69–70	.64[a]	.46[a]	.33[a]		
69–70/71–72	.57[a]	.48[a]	.33[a]		
71–72/73–74	.51[a]	.42[a]	.35[a]	.43	
73–74/75–76	.69[a]	.46[a]	.50[a]	.32	
75–76/77–78	.65[a]	.67[a]	.52[a]	.52[a]	
77–78/79–80	.83[a]	.76[a]	.70[a]	.75[a]	.75[a]

a. .001 level of significance.

ity in attention and the greater stability among older House incumbents demonstrate how allocation patterns stabilize over time; these patterns support Fenno's contention (1978) that home styles tend to harden over time. Like presentations of self and explanations of Washington activity, allocations of time to the district and state also tend to gain in consistency and stability.

INDIVIDUAL CHANGE

Fenno indentifies three types of individual circumstances that can induce members to change their home styles: contextual, strategic, and personal. "The most common contextual causes would be a redrawing of district boundaries and a marked population shift within old boundaries. The most common strategic cause would be a substantial decline in support among primary or reelection constituencies. The most common personal cause would be a shift in personal circumstances or goals. Singly or in combination, these factors probably produce home style change" (Fenno, 1978, p. 195). In terms of my study, I expect allocations of personal attention to constituency affairs to change in response to the existence of individual circumstances like those cited by Fenno. For example, the contextual circumstances of redistricting can change existing voter coalitions within the district and create the need to rebuild them. A logical response to redistricting would be to increase allocations of office and personal resources to constituency affairs in the hope of reconstructing a successful coalition in the redesigned district. If the displays of increased attention can endear congressmen to their constituents, this goal can be achieved without much difficulty. It would be expected, therefore, that redistricted congressmen would devote a greater proportion of their resources to the district than those who do not face redistricting. Such shifts in allocations would represent a significant change in home style toward greater attentiveness to the constituency.

Similarly, it is expected that members who experienced an electoral threat in their last election will devote more resources to their districts than those with safer margins in the previous election. The strategic cause of the change in resource allocations is the potential electoral threat that always shrouds marginal victories. The use of service to the district by legislators to broaden a minimally winning coalition leads to the expectation that electorally marginal incumbents will exhibit greater change in attention to the district than those with safer margins.

Finally, shifts in personal goals, as reflected in seeking higher office or retiring, could also induce changes in resource allocations that would qualify as change in home style. Incumbents who seek higher office might be expected to devote more resources to constituency affairs in order to increase their chances of winning that election by expanding their existing base of support. For instance, the more time spent in the district, the greater the opportunities for local media and newspaper coverage that can influence the perceptions of voters residing beyond district boundaries. Conversely, retiring members have little reason to increase the flow of resources to the district or state. In fact, the opposite would be expected; they would begin to scale down constituency activity as the date of retirement approached. Without a reelection battle to stimulate voter contact, the electoral incentive for attention to the constituency decreases. At the very least, the personal attention of the retiring incumbent to constituency affairs can be expected to decline, even if office contacts with constituents show no evidence of dissipating. Members who reduce their resource allocations to the district or state prior to retirement can be viewed as adopting less attentive home styles.

The research question underlying this stage of the analysis is the degree to which these individual circumstances can promote changes in the home styles of congressmen and senators.

Contextual Causes

In Table 8, I present figures for the mean levels of change in home style exhibited by incumbents in redistricted and non-redistricted states. I have separated a member's consecutive terms into pre- and post-redistricting periods so that I can estimate the intervening effects of redistricting on changes in attentiveness. For example, I have analyzed the changes in the periods surrounding the 1964 and 1966 implementations of state redistricting plans to see if changes in the time spent in the district can be attributed to these redistricting decisions. If redistricting can account for changes in style, some of the aggregate changes in attention illustrated in Figure 1 (chap. 1) could be attributed to the effects of redistricting during the 1960s and 1970s. The hypothesis that is being examined is that redistricting promotes changes in the allocation of resources, especially the personal attention that incumbents devote to constituency affairs.

It is clear from Table 8 that redistricting appears to have little effect on change in home style. There is no strong or significant difference between the levels of change exhibited by congressmen in redistricted and non-redistricted areas. In fact, in 1968 non-redistricted congressmen seem to have increased their levels of attention more than redistricted incumbents. The absence of a relationship between redistricting and change in style is subject to different interpretations. If one assumes that incumbents have a significant say in the drawing of their own congressional district lines, then redistricting may have resulted in less disruption to existing voter coalitions than might be expected. Therefore, incumbents may have had little need to adopt more attentive home styles.

Table 8
Redistricting and Change in Home Style

Year of Redistricting	Period of Change in Style	Mean Levels of Change Among Redistricted Congressmen	Mean Levels of Change Among Nonredistricted Congressmen
1964	1963–1964/1965–1966	27.1 (110)	22.7 (112)
1966	1965–1966/1967–1968	48.6 (29)	45.0 (195)
1968	1967–1968/1969–1970	16.9 (119)[a]	24.9 (134)
1970	1969–1970/1971–1972	− 2.9 (126)	1.2 (119)
1972	1971–1972/1973–1974	37.5 (19)	39.0 (228)

a. Statistically significant at .02 level.

Alternatively, redistricting may have lagged or anticipatory effects. The response of incumbents to a newly drawn district may be delayed because of the experimentation that accompanies expansionist behaviors. On the other hand, some incumbents may be able to anticipate their new district lines and adopt more attentive styles prior to the implementation of the redistricting plan. In either of these cases, redistricting effects might go unnoticed if one merely examines mean levels of change in style surrounding the implementation of a state's redistricting plan. It should be noted, however, that Fenno (1978, p. 195) failed to uncover an instance of a home-style change brought about by redistricting. This observation is consistent with the patterns in my data and reinforces the impression that redistricting has had little or no effect in promoting changes in attention.

Strategic Causes

Table 9 presents data relating to the effect of electoral marginality on the adoption of more attentive home styles. These data are divided according to whether a congressman received less than or more than 55 percent of the vote in the preceding election. This section of the analysis is restricted to representatives because of the problems involved in computing change in style over six-year periods for senators and because of the small number of senators available for analysis. The hypothesis is that marginal congressmen display greater changes in time spent in the constituency because their electoral marginality provides a forceful incentive for change. Therefore, one expects the mean levels of change in district attention to be higher for marginal victors than for their more electorally secure colleagues.

There is, however, little evidence in Table 9 to support this hypothesis since there are no significant differences in the levels of change between marginal and nonmarginal congressmen. This finding is not unexpected since most scholars investigating such linkages have been unable to find any traces of them (Johannes and McAdams, 1984; Parker and Parker, 1985b). Even though Fenno (1978, Table 2–1) also found electoral marginality to have no pronounced effect in increasing district travel, he suggests that the null findings may be a problem of conceptualization as well as of measurement.

Table 9
Electoral Threat and Change in Home Style Among Congressmen[a]

Previous Election	Period of Change in Style	Previous Election Won by Less than 55%	Previous Election Won by More than 55%
1964	1963–1964/1965–1966	28.1 (38)	24.2 (184)
1966	1965–1966/1967–1968	48.5 (19)	45.2 (205)
1968	1967–1968/1969–1970	16.7 (35)	21.9 (218)
1970	1969–1970/1971–1972	.6 (19)	− 1.0 (226)
1972	1971–1972/1973–1974	40.0 (24)	38.8 (223)
1974	1973–1974/1975–1976	14.0 (36)	20.6 (199)
1976	1975–1976/1977–1978	− 2.1 (29)	11.1 (246)
1978	1977–1978/1979–1980	44.2 (28)	29.0 (309)

a. None of the differences between the means reported in this table is statistically significant at .05 level.

It may be that our conventional indicators of electoral marginality are inadequate. Despite their extensive use, they have not helped to produce stable generalizations anywhere in the congressional literature. Perhaps objective measures that captured more electoral history, including primary election information, and took into account the member's career stage would prove superior. . . . Electoral statistics cannot capture the uncertainty members feel about their renomination and reelection. (Nor can they capture any existing sense of security among members in objectively marginal districts.) (Fenno, 1978, pp. 35–36)

Fenno also suggests that subjective assessments of electoral safety may be more valid indicators of marginality; he encourages scholars not to dismiss this hypothesis without further research. The plausibility of this proposition ensures the continued study of the hypothesized linkage between changes in home style and electoral threat. Nonetheless, I am firmly convinced that there is no simple and direct relationship between electoral marginality and changes in attention to constituency.

Personal Causes
I expect that a pending retirement from Congress would motivate senators to reduce the amount of time they spend in their states in the two-year term prior to retirement. In Table 10 I compare the mean number of days spent in the state for senators prior to retirement and for those running for reelection during the same period. Senators are grouped since the number retiring in any one election year is normally small, and this makes any inferences about their behavior problematic. Except for the first cohort of senators, who have retired in one of three successive elections (1960, 1962, or 1964), I have grouped senators who have retired in one of two consecutive elections.

The findings in Table 10 suggest that retiring senators may spend slightly less time in their states than those who are running for reelection, but the differences are relatively small, especially given the time frame examined (last two years of the senate term). This is the period during which senators generally intensify their home activities (especially if they are running for reelection), spending more time in their states and with constituents (Fenno, 1982; Taggert and Durant, 1984); hence incumbents running for reelection represent an unusu-

Table 10
Levels of Attention Among Senators Prior to Retirement

Senate Election	Mean Levels of Attention for Retiring Senators	Mean Levels of Attention for Senators Running for Reelection
1960–1964	8.2 (9)[a]	16.8 (86)
1966–1968	28.9 (9)	38.5 (51)
1970–1972	54.9 (8)	70.5 (48)
1974–1976	146.8 (15)	171.4 (45)
1978–1980	172.2 (12)	168.5 (44)

a. Number of senators upon which the means are based; senators from Maryland, Virginia, and Delaware are excluded from analysis.

ally attentive subset of senators during the term prior to the next election. Despite the high attentiveness of those running for another term, retiring senators compare favorably, spending similar amounts of time in their states in their last years of office. While this generalization is based upon a small number of cases, the evidence suggests that most senators do not let their home activities slip prior to their retirement.

There is also little empirical support for the hypothesized relationship between changes in attentiveness and retirement among representatives. Retiring congressmen actually increase their attention to their constituents prior to retirement. Except for 1970, the mean levels of change are all positive. This means that despite pending retirement, congressmen maintain or increase their levels of personal attention to constituency affairs. In fact, the levels of change among retiring congressmen are similar to those exhibited by all congressmen (Table 11). With the exceptions of 1964 and 1978,

Table 11
Retirement, Running for Higher Office, and Change in Home Style Among Congressmen

Last House Election	Period of Change	Mean Levels of Change in Style		
		Retiring Congressmen	Congressmen Seeking Higher Office	All Congressmen
1964	1963–1964/1965–1966	1.5 (4)	—	24.9 (222)
1966	1965–1966/1967–1968	55.2 (6)	77.2 (5)	45.5 (224)
1968	1967–1968/1969–1970	30.1 (18)	28.4 (13)	21.2 (253)
1970	1969–1970/1971–1972	– 9.2 (18)	3.3 (4)	– 0.9 (245)
1972	1971–1972/1973–1974	33.1 (28)	42.7 (6)	38.9 (247)
1974	1973–1974/1975–1976	17.5 (28)	50.9 (13)	19.6 (235)
1976	1975–1976/1977–1978	—	9.6 (10)	9.7 (275)
1978	1977–1978/1979–1980	14.8 (36)	7.4 (8)	30.3 (337)

there are rather small differences in the mean levels of change in home style exhibited by most members and by those about to retire. Retiring representatives and senators appear to maintain the same levels of personal attention to constituency affairs as other members.

The pattern is more ambiguous with respect to congressmen seeking higher office (senate or governorship). In two instances (1966 and 1974), they increased the time they spent in their districts beyond the level exhibited by all congressmen. In most instances (1968, 1970, 1972, and 1976), the differences are negligible; in 1978, there were far greater changes in attention for retiring congressmen than for their colleagues who sought higher office. In any event, there is no clear indication that running for higher office promotes changes in attention to the constituency.

In sum, there seems to be little convincing evidence that individual circumstances promote changes in the allocation of personal attention to constituency affairs. If pervasive individual circumstances, like redistricting, cannot produce individual change in resource allocations, it is unlikely that they can account for the aggregate changes in attention that one observes in Figure 1. Changes in home style may be sensitive to individual circumstances, as Fenno demonstrates (1978), but resource allocations appear to be largely unaffected by these forces.

CONCLUSIONS

It is not too surprising that home styles are difficult to change, since there are a variety of forces that promote stability in these styles. As I demonstrated with respect to one element of home style—the allocation of personal attention to constituency affairs—there is a large degree of stability in the resource allocations of senators and congressmen. Despite this consistency, allocations of personal attention exhibit change. But these are unaffected by individual circumstances such as redistricting, electoral marginality, or retirement.[2] One of the major reasons why individual circumstances may have so little effect on attention to the constituency is that changes in attentiveness have been widespread and uniform. If so, the effects of individual circumstances might be overwhelmed by systemwide changes in attention. This would minimize the potential for individual circumstances to effect changes in the time spent in the district or state. Institutional incentives may provide a better explanation for changes in the allocation of personal attention to constituency affairs. I examine the effects of institutional conditions in promoting change in home style in the next two chapters.

: 3 :

Aggregate Changes in Home Style

In the last chapter, I found little evidence that changes in the goals and electoral conditions of members promoted changes in the personal attentiveness of congressmen and senators. In this chapter, I examine aggregate changes in attentiveness to the constituency. Aggregate changes in home style capture the alterations in the behavior and attitudes of large numbers of congressmen or senators. As large proportions of the congressional membership alter their behavior in the same way, one should be able to identify both the existence of such aggregate changes and their causes.

In order to identify individual changes in attentiveness to the constituency (chap. 2), it was necessary to divide the data into categories reflecting individual conditions, such as retirement from Congress or running for higher political office. Comparisons were then made across these categories to determine the extent to which individual conditions could alter constituency activity. With aggregate changes in style, the forces that promote such changes arise from societal or institutional factors; hence my interest lies in associating aggregate changes in attentiveness with changes in societal or institutional variables. The causal explanation shifts from individual circumstances to institutional conditions.

Aggregate changes are more widespread than individual changes, although individual changes that affect large segments of Congress in the same way could also have systemic consequences. Since one of the basic premises of this study is that major changes in home style have occurred in Congress, such changes should be systemic in their origins and consequences and should be capable of generating widespread and significant behavioral changes. The breadth and significance of these behavioral changes mean that changes in home style should be visible in aggregate shifts in attentiveness.

Changes in the amount of time that congressmen and senators spend in their constituencies serve as the measure of change in style. While measurement of attentiveness is restricted to time spent in the district or state, other indicators of attentiveness display similar patterns of behavioral change. The growth in district offices (Fiorina, 1977) and the staff allocated to them (Schiff and Smith, 1983) are two examples of similar changes in attention to the constituency. Significant changes in the level of attention can be interpreted as evidence of home-style change in Congress—a pronounced and permanent shift on the part of incumbents toward a greater emphasis on constituency affairs.

POSSIBLE CAUSES OF AGGREGATE CHANGE

There are three possible explanations for the dynamics of aggregate change in home styles: cohort, period, and seniority effects. Each of these identifies a different mechanism for producing change in the home styles of congressmen and senators. Cohort effects (or generational replacement) promote change when new legislators differ on some major behavioral or attitudinal dimension from the members they replaced. A second feature of a cohort effect is that the source of change is generally common to all or most members of the generation or cohort. The political circumstances existing at the time of the election of a particular cohort might affect the way in which they view their legislative roles and responsibilities; this might be a source of discontinuity in behavior between newly elected members and those of longer tenure. For example, strong waves of national opinion, as might occur during a realigning election, can result in the entrance into Congress of members who represent a different ideological view from the one that was previously dominant. As members with the previously prevalent view are replaced by newer members with a different perspective, aggregate shifts would occur in the distribution of ideological beliefs within Congress. A third feature of cohort effects is that they persist over time. That is, in periods subsequent to the entry of the deviant cohort(s), one should continue to detect these differences.

In terms of our analysis, the generational replacement of less attentive congressmen and senators by more attentive ones could explain aggregate changes in attention to the constituency. This would be especially true during times when replacement was extensive. Such periods are fairly rare in recent electoral history, but congressional turnover in 1958, 1964, and 1974 was large by any standard of comparison; in senate elections, the "class of 1958" was one of the largest groups of newcomers. The unusual size of these freshman classes and their unusual electoral circumstances (many were minority party candidates who defeated incumbents from the majority party in that district or state) could serve to promote aggregate change in home style.

From this perspective, older members were not adopting more attentive styles as much as new members were bringing with them a new home style that emphasized attentiveness to the constituency. Thus, if the replacement of less attentive legislators by more attentive ones underlies the growth in attention to the constituency, one can expect to see differences between older and newer cohorts in the time they spend in their constituencies. More recent cohorts should spend greater amounts of time in their constituencies than older cohorts. A cohort explanation for increases in aggregate levels of attention discounts the degree to which these increases could result from the adoption of more attentive home styles on the part of older members. Admittedly, modification of an established home style, especially an electorally satisfying one, is an exception to the rule (Fenno, 1978). Nevertheless, such conversions do occur.

The conversion of older members to higher levels of attention to constituency is another source of aggregate change in style that is referred to as a period effect. The major characteristics of aggregate shifts that result from period effects are: First, changes cut across all generations and therefore involve conversion of behavior on the part of members already in the institution. Second, the changes are in the same direction for most members. Period effects generally result from stimuli that affect all members and induce a large proportion of them to respond in the same manner. Unlike cohort effects, which produce change in particular segments, period effects generally cause most members to change simultaneously. Systematic increases in the amount of time spent in the constituency on the part of most (or all) members of the House or Senate would be, perhaps, the most obvious way for aggregate changes in home style to occur. The important question to pose in regard to this type of change is what sorts of incentive could promote them, especially given the extent to which home styles tend to stabilize with the passage of time.

The regular increases in office allowances were of sufficient magnitude to have induced large numbers of congressmen and senators to adopt more attentive home styles. They could be expected to increase attention to constituency affairs as the level of the government subsidies for that activity increased, especially if these subsidies significantly reduced the costs associated with an attentive style. The result would be a uniform shift in aggregate levels of attention. In order for increases in travel allowances to be sources of change, each increase should precede a systematic shift in the attentiveness of incumbents, and changes should occur irrespective of seniority. In sum, the regular increases in the travel allowance could have led congressmen and senators to convert to higher levels of attentiveness, which would have resulted in aggregate changes in attention to the constituency.

Seniority effects occur as members move through institutionalized career patterns. That is, behavioral or attitudinal changes could accompany the occupation of certain positions in Congress. Lawrence Dodd (1977) suggests that such seniority or career-cycle effects are exhibited in the committee assignment process; members tend to transfer from the reelection committees they occupy at early points in their careers to more policy-oriented committees as their seniority increases. A seniority effect could also be conceptualized as underlying the attentiveness of legislators to their constituencies: they are attentive in the early terms of their careers, but they shift their efforts to the accomplishment of more personal goals as they gain congressional seniority. Junior members could be expected, therefore, to be more attentive to their constituents than older members, but these novices would reduce their levels of attention as they gained seniority. In fact, these attentive junior members should display the same level of attention as more senior members when similar levels of seniority are attained. Thus, if this type of effect were operative, incumbents would be expected to decrease their levels of attention as they gained seniority, the early years being devoted to extensive attention to the constituency. If there are career-cycle effects in the growth in attention to the constituency, the changes in style that appear are only transitory. Seniority effects might produce changes in aggregate levels of attention, but the changes would not reflect the sustained (and permanent) changes in attention that we expect of aggregate change in home style. Under these conditions, no change in style can be said to have occurred.

Therefore, rises in attention to the constituency could be associated with cohort, period, or seniority effects. The growth in attentiveness could be the result of generational replacement of less attentive incumbents by more attentive ones, the increases in the governmental subsidy for travel (travel allowance), and/or the movement of senators and congressmen through career cycles. The impact of these three processes may differ between the two chambers of Congress in generating change in home style. Cohort effects, for example, may be more significant in the House than in the Senate because of the greater frequency of congressional elections. In congressional elections large numbers of incumbents can be replaced, as in 1964 and 1974; under these circumstances, the cohort changes could amount to considerable aggregate changes in representational styles. Therefore, institutional differences, as well as similarities, might be expected in the processes that promote home-style changes.

Cohort Effects

The generational replacement of less attentive legislators by more attentive ones is the mechanism that explains how cohort effects might produce changes in aggregate levels of attentiveness. Replacement generations, or cohorts, can be viewed as bringing a different style of representation to the House or Senate—a style that emphasizes the extensive cultivation of constituents. There are two ways in which cohort effects might create the types of change in attentiveness that I term change in style. First, conditions at the time when a cohort enters Congress could structure their goals, motivations, or worldview. Entering classes of congressmen and senators are often characterized in terms of the societal or political conditions that existed at the time of their election. We speak of the "dovishness" of the Vietnam generations of congressmen, or the reform-minded nature of the Democrats from the "Watergate class." Morris Fiorina (1977), for example, suggests that the 1964 Democratic electoral landslide brought to Congress a number of new Democrats from previously Republican areas. Similar conditions also existed in the Senate at about the same time: an unusual number of northern Democrats were elected from largely Republican states in the late 1950s and early 1960s (Foley, 1980). These types of member could have adopted attentive home styles in order to build electoral support in these politically hostile areas.

Changes in the recruitment processes through which members enter Congress could also create aggregate changes in attention by shaping the new membership. The pressures and demands of life in Washington act as a screening process to eliminate certain types of individuals.[1] The political, social, and representational responsibilities that go along with being a member of Congress discourage still others from seeking and remaining in office. The financial support that is required to mount successful reelection campaigns further limits the types of candidates who seek to be and who are elected to the House and Senate. Thus some potential candidates eschew congressional office because of the built-in anxieties and pressures associated with representational roles; others are never elected because of the lack of sufficient funds and/or a receptive electorate.

In a similar way, decentralized political recruitment processes could also foster the selection of individuals who differ in ambition and goals from the majority of members already in Congress. James Payne argues that the "elite-managed method of entry" into Congress was replaced by more open and competitive mechanisms for recruitment in the 1950s. This change had a significant impact on the type of individual recruited for congressional contests. "The type of individual who won the approval of local elites through quiet labors and long term loyalty would tend to disappear. The modern system favors—indeed it almost requires—individuals who are tireless campaigners and zealous self-promoters. As a result, we would expect a greater proportion of such individuals—ambitious, publicity seeking types—to enter the House, especially after the early 1950s" (Payne, 1980, p. 477). Payne presents data demonstrating changes in the level of ambition exhibited by House members: the number of congressmen who retired to run for the Senate or a governorship doubled between 1954–1966 and 1968–1978 (ibid., p. 478). Such ambitious members, confronting an open and competitive electoral system, might be expected to pursue aggressively those constituency activities that would enhance their electoral safety and provide a measure of freedom from interference from the constituency.

There is some empirical support for attributing rises in the aggregate level of attention to the constituency to cohort or generational replacement effects. While Richard Fenno acknowledges the possibility that aggregate changes in home style might be induced by increases in the travel allowance (a period effect), he sees cohort effects as a more critical factor in promoting change.

Increased allowance and allotments have given veteran members an incentive to change home styles. So, both conversion and replacement seem to account for the increase in home attentiveness, whether measured by allocations for trips or staff. But, given the tendency of home styles to be established quickly and to persist over time, it is our guess that replacement—the infusion of more home-oriented freshmen—is the more important factor in producing aggregate stylistic change. (Fenno, 1978, p. 209)

Steven Schiff and Steven Smith find a similar pattern in the use of congressional staff. They analyzed the distribution of congressional office staff between the Washington and district offices following each increase in the staff allowance and concluded that: "the acquisition, distribution, and use of staff by the new generation of House members appears to have enabled them to pursue more vigorously both Washington and constituency career objectives. While larger staffs add problems of management to members' burdens, . . . they also enable members to be . . . more attentive to their constituencies" (Schiff and Smith, 1983, p. 465). The evidence that recent congressional generations are more attentive to their constituencies than older cohorts suggests that cohort differences might exist in the amount of time that incumbents spend in their districts and states.

To generate a sufficient number of cases for the analysis of generational effects in attentiveness, I have grouped cohorts into six-year periods. The staggering of senate elections necessitates this strategy; grouping reduces the possible impact of the particular blend of states that have senate elections during any single two-year period on the differences between cohorts. That is, all states will have had both senate elections during a six-year period. While there is less of a need to combine House cohorts into six-year periods, the same categorization will be performed for both chambers to facilitate comparisons that are essential to understanding the dynamics of home-style change in Congress. Incumbents are grouped into the following five cohorts: those elected (1) before 1958, (2) between 1958 and 1963, (3) between 1964 and 1969, (4) between 1970 and 1975, and (5) between 1976 and 1980.[2]

This cohort classification serves a number of analytic purposes: first, it enables one to monitor the home styles of congressmen and senators who entered Congress before and after increases in the travel allowance. This provides the opportunity to examine the degree to which older members converted to higher levels of attention to the constituency. The classification also divides members into groups that are associated with unusual conditions at the time of entry into Congress. For instance, classes of congressmen and senators associated with unusual partisan turnover have been isolated: senators elected between 1958 and 1963, congressmen elected between 1964 and 1969, and cohorts elected during the 1970s.[3] Clearly, some individual cohorts may be more useful than others in identifying cohort changes because the conditions of their entry were more dramatic. Senators elected, for example, in 1958 were probably more unusual in terms of their party identifications and the electoral histories of their states than those elected in 1962. While my groupings might obscure some of the specific cohort differences that exist, this is not a problem since I have examined individual cohort classes to ensure that the patterns in attentiveness are similar across categories. Hence I am confident that I have identified reliable patterns of cohort changes.

Period Effects

Aggregate changes in attentiveness to the constituency could also result from increases in the travel allowances. These increases could induce members to adopt more attentive home styles, irrespective of their seniority, for at least two related reasons. First, viewed as rational actors (Mayhew, 1974a), congressmen and senators might be expected to exploit the resources of their offices. Certainly, this is the assumption that underlies much of the research that attempts to link electoral safety and perquisite usage (Cover, 1977; Born, 1982; Cover and Brumberg, 1982). Second, the increases can be viewed as shaping the opportunity structure by creating incentives that encouraged members to spend greater amounts of time in their constituencies. As the government subsidy for travel increased and the legislative schedule was systematically adjusted to accommodate its use (chap. 4), the incentives for members to spend greater amounts of time in their constituencies also grew. Therefore, congressmen and senators could be expected to respond to increases in the travel allowance by spending more time in their constituencies. The consequence would be a conversion to higher levels of attention and an aggregate increase in attention.

One can find both similarities and differences in the legislative histories surrounding increases in the House and Senate travel allowances. For instance, Senate and House allowances were increasing during the same period, roughly between 1965 and 1973. House allowances, however, continued to increase after Senate allowances had already stabilized (Table 12). Table 12 also shows that the increases in the House allowances were more frequent than those in the Senate allowances and that a higher level of government subsidy is at present attached to House travel allowances. For example, Senate travel allotments now provide for about 20 round trips to the state while House allotments permit 32 round trips to the district. These differing levels could partially explain the higher levels of attentiveness displayed by House incumbents, though it seems unlikely. Therefore, if changes in attentiveness are produced by increases in the travel allowances, the conversion of members to higher levels of attention should follow these increases and be relatively uniform across cohorts.

Seniority Effects

Some, if not all changes in attention could be merely transitory, reflecting career-cycle experiences. Changes in attention to constituency may reflect the shifting priorities of congressmen and senators

Table 12
Increases in Travel Allowances

	Travel Allotment (per year)	Public Law	Effective Date
Senate	2	PL 85–570	July 1, 1958
	6	PL 89–90	July 1, 1965
	12	PL 91–145	July 1, 1969
	Unlimited (based on 20–22 round trips in calculating allocation)	PL 92–51	July 1, 1971
		PL 92–607 (1972)[a]	January 1, 1973
House of Representatives	2	PL 88–70	July 1, 1963
	4	PL 89–147	August 28, 1965
	12	PL 90–86	January 3, 1967
	18	Committee Order 2[b]	January 3, 1973
	26	Committee Order 19	May 20, 1975
	32	Decision of the Committee on House Administration	January 3, 1978

a. The travel allowance was consolidated with other allowances in October 1972.
b. Public Law 92–184 gave authority to the Committee on House Administration to fix and adjust transportation allowances from time to time; hence further changes in the travel allotment are issued by Committee Orders.

as they gain seniority. With seniority comes power, influence, and broader legislative interests; the zero-sum nature of a member's own time means that some obligations suffer. As seniority increases, so do party and institutional responsibilities. Leadership positions require greater attention to the time-consuming duties associated with policy formation and coalition building. Further, positions of legislative power require attention to nationwide groups and causes that also detract from the amount of attention that can be spent in cultivating constituents. Under these conditions, the first demand on a member's time that is likely to be reduced is the personal time spent in the district or state.

As the interest in cultivating the district or state begins to wane, incumbents are susceptible to familiar attacks of "forgetting about the folks back home," or "ignoring fence-mending" responsibilities. Donald Matthews suggests that just such a political career-cycle operates in the Senate.

If the senator survives the first challenge to his position, then he becomes more secure than before. All the advantages he possessed at the first re-election bid are even more compelling now. But with greater seniority and security go additional legislative responsibilities. By the end of his second term, he is, in all likelihood, a senior member of major committees. He is well on the way to becoming an important national figure, increasingly concerned with pressing national and international problems. In the vocabulary of social psychology, his "reference groups" change, he becomes more concerned with Senate, national, and international problems, and devotes less time and attention to the folks back home. The press of legislative duties becomes ever harder to escape. Advancing years make fence-mending trips increasingly onerous. (Matthews, 1973, p. 242)

Thus seniority should diminish attention to the constituency: the increases in attention that appear are only temporary and created by initial electoral insecurities. The transitory nature of the changes produced by seniority effects precludes these types of change from being considered as *permanent* changes in attentiveness.

There are a number of examples of seniority or career-cycle effects on members' behavior, especially with respect to perquisite usage. Richard Born, for example, examined the utilization of office staff and district offices by House incumbents between 1960 and

1976. He concludes that the differences among congressmen appeared to be a function of seniority.

Thus, after about three terms, new generation members no longer demonstrate any of the special aggressiveness that characterized their initial freshman period of service. Instead, there actually is a rather rapid relaxation in their labors as seniority accumulates. Cohorts of the new and old generation, then, chiefly are distinguished by differences in the intensity of constituent-directed activity arising during the first term of incumbency. (Born, 1982, p. 357)

Albert Cover found a similar pattern in the levels of congressional mailings. Analyzing the number of mass mailings distributed by a sample of congressmen to their constituents, he found that the level of communication was related to seniority. He suggested the following explanations for these seniority effects:

Perhaps senior members require a less aggressive communications effort because their views are sought out by local or national media. Or perhaps they feel that their constituents have learned enough about them over time to make a vigorous effort relatively profitless. After several terms in Congress, members may assume that they are well acquainted with constituency opinion, thus reducing their incentive to send out questionnaires soliciting information from constituents. Of course, senior members may simply be too busy with other matters to worry very much about mass mailings. As members move into positions of influence in the House, they almost inevitably withdraw some of their time and attention from constituents. (Cover, 1980, p. 131)

Each of these explanations for increases in attentiveness predicts a different pattern of change in attention. Nonetheless, cohort, period, and seniority effects are entangled with one another. That is, seniority is a perfect function of cohort membership and period. Cohort membership is a perfect function of seniority and period; and period is a perfect function of seniority and cohort membership. Stated differently, the effects of cohort, period, and seniority are each linearly dependent on the other two. Therefore, a research strategy must be employed that will make it possible to differentiate among cohort, period, and seniority effects in the amount of time that legislators spend in their constituencies.

THE DIFFERENTIATION OF COHORT, PERIOD, AND
SENIORITY EFFECTS

The problem of separating cohort, period, and seniority effects is often ignored in contemporary research on Congress, although this neglect could result in dubious, if not fallacious, arguments and conclusions. For instance, period and cohort effects could be "disguised" as seniority influences. Frequently, scholars obtain measurements of differing behaviors that are either cross-sectional or longitudinal in nature. Researchers either measure the differences between cohorts at the same point in time (cross-sectional differences), or differences within the same cohort over time (longitudinal differences). Inferences based upon cross-sectional differences cannot, by themselves, differentiate between seniority and cohort effects, nor can inferences from longitudinal comparisons distinguish between seniority and period effects. This is not merely the result of data limitations. The separation of cohort, period, and seniority effects is possible only under certain conditions or assumptions. In the next few pages I describe conditions necessary for separating these effects, and the ways in which one can identify the processes underlying changes in home style. My methodological approach to this question is guided by the research strategy developed by Erdman Palmore (1978) for separating cohort, period, and seniority effects.

Differences in attentiveness can be measured in three ways: as longitudinal, cross-sectional, or time-lag differences. Longitudinal differences are those between earlier and later measurements of the attentiveness of the same cohort. Cross-sectional differences are those between the attentiveness of older and younger cohorts at the same point in time. Finally, time-lag differences are those between the attentiveness of an older cohort after a certain amount of time in Congress and a later measurement of younger cohorts after the same amount of time. Each of these observable differences is composed of only two effects: "Age [seniority] effects are reflected in longitudinal and cross-sectional differences. Period effects are reflected in longitudinal and time-lag differences. Cohort effects are reflected in cross-sectional and time-lag differences" (ibid., p. 285). This explains why valid inferences cannot be made on the basis of any single type of observed difference: each observable difference is composed of two possible effects. Patterns in these differences, however, provide additional evidence that aids in distinguishing the impact of one influence from that of another.

There are three basic patterns of observable differences that can be obtained from these data: no significant differences, two significant differences, and three significant differences. The significance of the differences in attention to constituency can be identified on the basis of their statistical probability (i.e., statistical tests of significance); I have chosen a stringent level of statistical significance (alpha < .001) to ensure that I am not uncovering unimportant or marginal shifts in attentiveness. When longitudinal, cross-sectional, and time-lag differences in the amount of time spent in the district or state are not significantly different from what one might expect on the basis of chance, the most likely inference is that there is no evidence of cohort, period, or seniority effects.

If two of the three differences are statistically significant, then one is justified in inferring that only a single effect is present and reflected in the existence of two types of significant difference. The identification of the effect that underlies the two types of difference can be made by noting which effect is common to the two significant differences:

Longitudinal and Cross-Sectional Differences = Seniority Effects
Cross-Sectional and Time-Lag Differences = Cohort Effects
Longitudinal and Time-Lag Differences = Period Effects

Thus, if a political career-cycle underlies the growth in attentiveness, one should find both longitudinal and cross-sectional differences in the time that incumbents spend in their constituencies. If changes in attentiveness are a function of the conversion of older cohorts to greater attentiveness, we should find both longitudinal and time-lag differences. Finally, if the growth in attentiveness to the constituency is due to the replacement of less attentive congressmen and senators by more attentive ones, one should observe both cross-sectional and time-lag differences.

Inferences are the most problematic when one uncovers longitudinal, cross-sectional, *and* time-lag differences in attention. Unless there are other grounds for assuming that one of the effects is not present (cohort, period, or seniority), one cannot separate the three influences or estimate their individual effects. One needs to examine additional information under this condition (i.e., three significant differences) to be able to make inferences as to the causes of changes in home style.[4] It is necessary to look for evidence that one of the three effects is unlikely to be present. The statistical significance of the observed differences will be determined by t-tests and F-tests (ANOVA).

Aggregate Change in the Senate

Table 13 shows the mean number of days spent by senators in their states between 1959 and 1980. These data are organized by Congress and by cohort classes divided into six-year periods. As one moves from Congress to Congress in Table 13, it is evident that the amount of time that senators have spent in their states has increased significantly over time. For example, during the 86th Congress (1959–1960), they averaged about 7–8 days a session in their states; the mean number of days increased to 18 with the first increase in the Senate travel allowance in 1965. This increase in attention continues until the 94th Congress (1975–1976). Since there are significant differences in attention (Table 13), one may safely conclude that the differences are a result of cohort, period, or seniority effects. That is, one can reject the hypothesis that none of these effects is present. The question now is to determine the extent to which cohort, period, or seniority effects can explain the changes.

The only statistically significant relationships in Table 13 are the longitudinal differences that follow changes in the travel allowance: 1965–1966, 1969–1970, 1973–1974. During the 89th Congress (1965–1966), senators' attentiveness increased from about 18 days to 36 days; during the 91st Congress (1969–1970), it increased to about 70 days. The last significant change occurred during the 93rd Congress (1973–1974), when the number of days that senators spent in their states increased to about 144 days. T-tests for paired samples were performed for pairs of successive Congresses (i.e., two-year periods) with a one-tailed test of significance. T-values were significant (alpha < .001 level) only at these three time points, and there were no significant differences in the time spent in the state in any period since the 1973–1974 period, when travel allowances were last increased. The cross-sectional differences in state attention were analyzed, but none were found to be statistically significant, although senators elected during the 1970s tend to spend more time in their states than those elected in earlier periods.

The time-lag differences in state attentiveness (Table 14) indicate that senators, at the same points in their careers, spend different amounts of time in their states: newer cohorts of senators spend more time in their states than older senators did when they were at that level of seniority. For instance, members elected during the 1970s spent twice as much time in their states after their first term in the Senate as those elected between 1964 and 1969, and eight times as much as those elected before 1963. After two terms, senators elected between 1964 and 1969 were also spending twice as much time in their states at those elected before this period.

The existence of longitudinal and time-lag differences in attention provide the evidence necessary for determining which effect can best account for changes in attentiveness: period effects. Seniority and cohort effects require evidence of cross-sectional differences, but none of these differences attain statistical significance. Nor is there any evidence that a nonlinear, cross-sectional relationship might underlie cohort effects.[5] The lack of such differences leads one to reject the possibility that increases in attention to the state are the result of cohort or seniority effects. In sum, changes in the time spent by senators seem best explained by their conversion to higher levels of attention as a result of increases in the travel allowance.

It should be clear that the levels of change in attention are as substantial as they are significant (Table 15). The change in the travel allowance during the 91st Congress (1969–1970) from 6 to 12 round trips to the state resulted in an increase of nearly 28 days per Congress (almost an extra month) in the state. The most recent increase in the travel allowance (1973–1974) to about 20 round trips resulted in an additional 60 days spent in the state during that Congress, or about two extra months. Thus the increases in the travel allowance have had significant and substantial effects on aggregate changes in attention to the state.

This is not to deny the force of the motivations for changes in attention that existed among senators and guided the expansion of the travel allowance. It seems unlikely, however, that the magnitude and breadth of the aggregate changes that are observed would have occurred in the absence of the expansion of subsidies for attention to

Table 13
Mean Number of Days Spent in the State per Congress by Senate Cohort, 1959–1980

Years/ Mean	Year Elected (Senate Cohort)				
	Before 1958	1958–1963	1964–1969	1970–1975	1976–1979
1959–1960 15.5	15.2 (71)[a]	16.7 (20)			
1961–1962 14.5	15.5 (62)	12.6 (31)			
1963–1964 17.9	16.8 (52)	19.4 (41)			
1965–1966 35.8	31.6[b] (49)	38.8[b] (38)	46.5 (8)		
1967–1968 42.4	40.6 (46)	44.0 (36)	44.0 (13)		

1969–1970 69.9	75.6[b] (35)	59.1[b] (33)	76.2[b] (26)		
1971–1972 82.6	88.1 (32)	78.0[b] (29)	67.1 (24)	119.2 (9)	
1973–1974 143.7	143.3[b] (26)	143.8[b] (25)	138.4[b] (22)	149.8 (20)	
1975–1976 138.4	123.0 (20)	141.6 (24)	123.7 (19)	155.0 (31)	
1977–1978 154.8	154.7 (14)	145.1 (17)	114.9 (16)	188.4 (27)	148.8 (17)
1979–1980 168.2	173.2 (10)	159.7 (15)	134.1 (12)	183.0 (22)	172.9 (35)

Source: Travel vouchers submitted to the secretary of the Senate. Excludes senators from Delaware, Maryland, and Virginia and senators who did not complete a full term.

a. Number of senators in that cohort at that time period.

b. .001 level of significance of longitudinal difference (t-test).

Table 14
Time-Lag Differences in Time Spent in the State (mean number of days)

Number of Terms	Senate Cohorts		
	1958–1963	1964–1969	1970–1975
1	19.4	76.2	155.0
2	59.1	123.7	

Source: Travel vouchers of U.S. senators, 1959–1980. Table compiled from table 13.

the constituency such as travel. For instance, it is clear that attention to the state did not increase significantly between increases in the travel allowance, and newer members appear to be no more attentive than older ones. Therefore, there is little evidence that changes in the attentiveness of senators would have occurred in the absence of increases in the travel allowance. Increased subsidies provided a necessary incentive for such changes. Without these perquisites, incumbents had little reason to increase their attentiveness, especially since an increased presence in the state represents a financial drain, as well as a psychological one, on the member. The travel subsidy, like other perquisites, helped to reduce the costs of attention and facilitated a permanent change in the home styles of incumbents.

Aggregate Change in the House

Table 16 shows the mean number of days that representatives spent in their districts between 1963 and 1980.[6] I have organized these data like those concerning senators to facilitate comparisons. These data are organized by Congress and cohort classes that are divided into the same six-year periods as the data for senators. Like senators, congressmen have significantly increased the amount of time that they spend in their constituencies. Although congressmen are considerably more attentive than senators, the rise in attention to the district appears to follow the same pattern as that in attention to the state: significant rises in the amount of time spent in the constituency between the 89th (1965–1966) and the 93rd (1973–1974)

Table 15
Magnitude of Change in Attention to the State[a]

Period of Significant Change	Increase from Previous Congress		Increase from Last Period of Significant Change		Number of Trips Permitted
	Days	%	Days	%	
1965–1966	17.9	100	—	—	6
1969–1970	27.5	65	34.1	95	12
1973–1974	61.1	74	73.8	106	20

Source: Travel vouchers of U.S. senators, 1959–1980. Table compiled from table 13.
a. Entries are the mean number of days spent in the state by all senators.

Table 16
Mean Number of Days Spent in the District per Congress by House Cohort, 1963–1980

Years/ Mean	Year Elected (House Cohort)				
	Before 1958	1958–1963	1964–1969	1970–1975	1976–1979
1963–1964 16.5	17.5 (191)[a]	15.5 (162)			
1965–1966 40.0	40.2[b] (128)	40.1[b] (109)	39.5 (76)		
1967–1968 84.8	79.6[b] (98)	84.4[b] (96)	90.7[b] (95)		
1969–1970[c] 107.4	97.9[b] (88)	109.4[b] (85)	113.3[b] (113)		
1971–1972[c] 106.9	98.0 (80)	110.1 (71)	110.0 (113)	110.1 (39)	

1973–1974[c] 150.0	122.9[b] (60)	151.6[b] (71)	154.0[b] (99)	162.0[b] (92)	
1975–1976[c] 176.4	136.1 (45)	161.2 (50)	176.4[b] (77)	192.8[b] (157)	
1977–1978[c] 197.2	129.6 (43)	192.1 (59)	191.2 (80)	209.3 (158)	224.2 (66)
1979–1980[c] 235.5	169.8 (29)	222.5[d] (47)	238.4[b] (65)	228.8[b] (130)	259.1[b] (136)

Source: Travel vouchers submitted to the clerk of the House. Excludes congressmen from Delaware, Maryland, and Virginia and congressmen who did not complete a full term.

a. Number of congressmen in that cohort at that time period.

b. .001 level of significance of longitudinal difference (t-test).

c. .001 level of significance of cross-sectional differences (ANOVA).

d. Statistically significant longitudinal difference between 1973–1974 and 1979–1980.

Congresses. However, changes in the attentiveness of representatives continue throughout the series, whereas changes in the attentiveness of senators generally subside after 1974. The magnitude of change also seems to be greater for House than Senate incumbents. In the 1963–1964 period, senators and congressmen were spending about the same number of days, an average of about 8 per session, in their constituencies (Tables 13 and 16). During the 96th Congress (1979–1980), senators were spending about 84 days per session, but congressmen were spending more than 100 days per session, or more than 1 of every 4 days, in their constituencies. These institutional differences lead one to suspect that the rises in attentiveness on the part of congressmen are caused by more than the increases in the travel allowance.

There are three types of statistically significant differences that can be observed in the changes over time in attention to the district: longitudinal, cross-sectional, and time-lag differences. The existence of significant longitudinal differences (Table 16) indicates that there has been a relatively uniform shift in the attentiveness of House incumbents at these time periods. That is, most members increase the time that they spend in their districts by the same amount. The significant cross-sectional differences suggest that since the late 1960s (1969–1970), recent generations of congressmen have been more attentive to their districts than older generations (those elected before 1958). And each successive House cohort seems to be somewhat more attentive than past ones, though the differences are slight in most instances. Finally, the time-lag differences in attention mean that newer generations of congressmen are spending more time in their constituencies than older congressmen did at the same points in their congressional careers. The existence of longitudinal, cross-sectional, and time-lag differences provides evidence for rejecting the possibility that changes in attentiveness cannot be explained by cohort, period, or seniority effects.

Analysis of changes in the attentiveness of congressmen is more difficult than that of changes in the attention of senators because three types of differences are apparent in the former. As I noted earlier, conclusions about the forces that underlie changes in attention are most problematic when there are significant longitudinal, cross-sectional, *and* time-lag differences. Under such circumstances, it is necessary to examine additional information for evidence that one of the effects—cohort, period, or seniority—is least likely to effect changes in attentiveness.

I find no evidence in Table 16 that seniority effects are present: in every cohort, House incumbents increase rather than decrease the amount of time they spend in their congressional districts. This conclusion is bolstered by the fact that the oldest cohort (those elected before 1958) exhibit significant increases rather than decreases in attentiveness as their seniority increases. This generation is one that might be expected to respond to seniority effects, and their increased attention serves as a sharp contradiction to what one would expect if seniority effects were present. For these reasons, the possibility that increased seniority reduces attention is rejected. I assume that the changes in attention to the district can be explained by generational and period effects alone.

Longitudinal changes in attention to the district are evident at six time spans (Table 16). In four of these, 1965–1966, 1967–1968, 1969–1970, and 1973–1974, the longitudinal differences are statistically significant across all cohorts. In the other two, 1975–1976 and 1979–1980, where we find evidence of longitudinal differences in attention, the differences are primarily significant among those elected after 1964. In five of the six instances of longitudinal differences, the changes can be associated with increases in the travel allowance. The only exception is the change in attentiveness that occurred in the 91st Congress (1969–1970). While no increase in the travel allowance occurred during this time, the dramatic one that took place during the previous Congress (1967–1968) may have prompted a prolonged change in attention to the district. Between the 89th and 90th Congresses, the allowance increased from 4 round trips to 12. This increase had a dramatic impact on the attentiveness of House incumbents, resulting in more than a 100 percent increase in the amount of time spent in the district in the following Congress (Table 18). One might expect that the size of this increase in the travel allowance, which tripled the previous allocation, might produce changes that persist for a time; clearly, no other increase in the travel allotment represents such a dramatic shift in the governmental subsidy for travel to the district.

Aside from the longitudinal differences in attention, time-lag dif-

Table 17
Time-Lag Differences in Time Spent in the District by Congressmen (mean number of days)

	House Cohorts		
Number of Terms	1964–1969	1970–1975	1976–1979
1	39.5	110.1	224.2
2	90.7	162.0	259.1
3[a]	*113.3*	*192.8*	
4	110.0	209.3	
5	154.0	228.8	

Source: Travel vouchers of U.S. congressmen, 1963–1980. Table compiled from table 16.

a. Palmore (1978) suggests that the most appropriate time-lag differences are those where the number of years between early and later measurements are equal to the number of years in the range of each cohort (six years). Thus the time-lag differences after three terms of service are the relevant differences to be examined (italicized). This pattern is repeated in the time-lag differences at other points in time.

ferences are also evident. As Table 17 demonstrates, there are substantial differences in the attentiveness of members at the same points in their congressional careers: cohorts elected during the 1970s are considerably more attentive to their districts than those elected between 1964 and 1969, and the most recent generation (those elected between 1976 and 1979) are even more attentive to their constituents than previous generations. The association of longitudinal differences in attention with increases in the travel allowance, and the existence of time-lag differences in attention, suggest that changes in attention exhibit period effects.

Thus there is strong evidence that the increases in the travel allowance helped to promote changes in attention. This conversion to higher levels of attention to the district occurred at about the same time as senators were exhibiting similar changes, 1965–1974. Unlike the attentiveness of senators, there is some evidence of additional period effects in that of congressmen after 1974: during the 94th (1975–1976) and 96th (1979–1980) Congresses, the most recent generations of congressmen increased their attention to their districts in response to increases in the travel allowance during these Congresses (Table 16). House incumbents elected before 1958, however, exhibit no further significant increases in attention after 1974, despite additional increases in the travel allowance.

One can only speculate as to why recent increases in the travel allowance had little effect on older congressmen. One might attribute this generational difference to the conditions that existed at the time when successive generations of congressmen were entering the institution. Representatives elected after 1964 were entering Congress at the same time as perquisites were increasing. As I demonstrate in the next chapter, a variety of perquisites that were designed to help the member keep in contact with constituents were being established or expanded at that time. House members elected then may have found it easier to adjust their home styles to the expanded opportunities for contact with constituents. The individualistic nature of home styles and the extent to which they solidify over time may make members who entered Congress before the expansion of perquisites less willing (or able) to exploit the additional resources for contact with constituents. After all, the electoral survival of these members is evidence of the development of a successful home style. Why tamper with success?

In addition to the period effects, aggregate changes in attention appear to exhibit cohort or generational effects. Such cohort effects are far more pronounced in the House than in the Senate. In the House, cross-sectional differences in attention appear at every Congress after 1968, whereas there is no evidence of such differences for senators. The absence of this type of difference led to the conclusion that changes in style would not have occurred among senators but for the increases in the travel allowance. The existence of cross-sectional differences in congressmens' attention suggests that changes in attentiveness could have transpired in the House through the replacement of less attentive members by more attentive ones. In short, cohort effects appear to be another mechanism through which aggregate changes in attentiveness might occur in the House.

The cross-sectional differences in attentiveness and the time-lag differences that were discussed earlier suggest the existence of cohort effects in attention to the district since 1968. At each time span after 1968, cohorts elected since 1958 are significantly more attentive than those elected earlier. For example, in 1980 House incumbents elected before 1958 averaged about 85 days per session in their districts compared with more than 100 days per session for those elected after 1958. As I noted earlier, each successive generation of House members appears to be somewhat more attentive than earlier cohorts, but the differences are small in most instances.

One explanation for the timing of the generational differences in attention to the district is suggested by Fiorina's speculation regarding the factors promoting the decline in marginal congressional seats during the 1960s. He suggests that the rise in incumbent electoral safety in the 1960s can be attributed to the election of members in the mid-1960s who "placed relatively greater emphasis on constituency service than those whom they replaced" (Fiorina, 1977, pp. 54–55). This suggests that the differences in attention could be due to the generational replacement of less attentive congressmen by more attentive ones in the mid-1960s. This is an accurate characterization in the sense that those elected at that time did spend more time in their districts than those they replaced. There are, however, two reasons for rejecting this explanation for the timing of the generational differences in attentiveness. First, the differences did not appear until 1969; hence the infusion of more attentive congressmen in the mid-1960s did not produce any generational differences with their entrance into Congress. Second, the generational differences that do appear in 1969–1970 differentiate between members elected before and after 1958, not 1964. During most of the Congresses, there are only small differences in the attentiveness of successive cohorts elected after 1958. While those elected during the mid-1960s were more attentive than those they replaced, they were not more attentive to their districts than those elected six years earlier. In sum, the infusion of more "home-oriented" congressmen in the mid-1960s cannot alone explain the timing of the generational differences in attention since the entrance of this cohort did not create additional generational differences.

The existence of period effects prior to the appearance of cohort effects suggests a socialization explanation for the emergence of cohort differences in attentiveness: the electoral success that resulted from the conversion of members to higher levels of attention in the mid-1960s prompted those confronting electoral uncertainties to pursue constituency activities more aggressively. The electoral value of an attentive style became congressional lore, and, in a very real sense, the lesson was passed on from generation to generation.[7] Today, there is no more widely held belief than that attention to constituency affairs enhances electoral safety. I reiterate: I can only speculate about the timing of the generational effects that I observe on district attention, but my analysis demonstrates that increases in the travel allowance preceded cohort differences.

Finally, it should be evident that the level of change is substantial as well as significant (Table 18). When the travel allowance was raised from 2 to 4 round trips in 1965, House incumbents increased time spent in the district by about 20 days (per two-year period); when the allowance was raised from 4 to 12 round trips, they increased the time by over 20 days per session; when the allowance was raised from 12 to 18 round trips, they increased the time by an additional 20 days.

The existence of period effects and generational differences in attention indicate that both conversion and replacement are involved in the aggregate changes that are observed among House members. Older members have converted to higher levels of attention as Congress increased the travel allotment, and less attentive members have gradually been replaced by more attentive ones. It should also be noted that during the time of home-style change in *both* the House and the Senate (1965–1974), period effects had a greater impact than generational effects on aggregate changes.[8] After 1974 period effects lose their influence and cohort effects become the dominant factor in producing change in the House. Period effects, therefore, appear to be influential in producing changes in home style, but their influence has declined as most change in style in the House is at present being produced by the replacement of less attentive members by more attentive ones.

CONCLUSIONS

There are a number of similarities in changes in attentiveness between House and Senate incumbents. For example, there is no evidence that either House or Senate members decrease their attention

Table 18
Magnitude of Change in Attention to the District[a]

Period of Significant Change	Increase from Previous Congress		Increase from Last Period of Significant Change		Number of Trips Permitted
	Days	%	Days	%	
1965–1966	23.4	141	—	—	4
1967–1968	44.8	112	44.8	112	12
1969–1970	22.6	27	22.6	27	12
1973–1974	43.1	40	42.6	40	18
1975–1976	26.4	18	26.4	18	26
1979–1980	38.3	19	59.1	34	32

Source: Travel vouchers of U.S. congressmen, 1963–1980. Table compiled from table 16.

a. Entries are the mean number of days spent in the district by all congressmen.

to constituency affairs as they gain seniority. Time spent in the constituency is hard work for most members, and those wishing to disengage from their commitments in the constituency would find the reduction in the time spent a major method of doing so. Most members, however, appear to increase the time they spend in their constituencies during the span of the analysis. Further, changes in style among senators and congressmen reflect the effects of the increases in the travel allowance. These period effects induced aggregate patterns of change in attentiveness at about the same time in the House and Senate—between 1965 and 1974.

There is an alternative interpretation of the relationship between time spent in the state or district and increases in the travel allowance (i.e., of period effects). Specifically, it might be argued that the association is only an artifact of more complete filings of travel vouchers. According to this proposition, incumbents have not actually increased the amount of time they spend in their states or districts but continue to spend the same amount of time today as they did two or three decades earlier; the only thing that has changed has been the level of government subsidy of such travel— as the travel allowance increased, incumbents just filed more vouchers to gain reimbursement for travel that had previously been financed from other funds.

This proposition is untenable for two reasons. First, while congressmen have maintained "unofficial" office accounts until very recently, the best available information suggests that few used them to finance their travel to their own district: a survey of House members and their staffs conducted by the Obey Commission in the late 1970s found that only 12 percent of those who admitted that they maintained such accounts used them for travel to their districts (U.S. Congress, 1977, p. 927). While some members may have paid for travel to their constituency from other funds, the number who admit to doing so are few. It also seems unlikely that such a small group of individuals could produce significant aggregate longitudinal changes in attention to constituency.

Second, Richard Fenno's study (1978) of the travel of congressmen to their districts reveals changes in attention that are similar to those reported in my study although he relied upon interviews with administrative assistants and personal secretaries rather than vouchers for information.[9] As for the Senate, the unpublished study by Dorothy

Cronheim (1957, p. 129) cited by Fenno, provides similar survey evidence of changes in attention to constituency. "Cronheim inquired of senatorial assistants how often senators went home in 1956. Of the fifty-two interview replies, thirty-nine senators went home ten times a year or less, and thirteen went home more than ten times a year" (Fenno, 1978, p. 212). Cronheim's estimates depart radically from the amount of time that senators are spending in their states at present. Therefore, the picture remains the same whether analyzed in terms of the vouchers filed or of the estimates made by a member's staff: congressmen and senators have increased the amount of time they have spent in their districts or states during recent decades.

The major difference in changes between representatives and senators is the appearance of cohort effects in the House. Whereas more recent cohorts of congressmen are more attentive to their districts than older generations, there is no significant generational difference in the attentiveness of senators. This institutional difference probably reflects the effects of the differences in the term of office. That is, the two-year congressional term probably exaggerates for new members the insecurities associated with elections.

I also observe institutional differences in the levels of attention exhibited by House and Senate incumbents. Representatives are considerably more attentive to their constituencies than senators. In fact, they appear to exploit their resources to a larger extent than senators. For instance, in 1965–1966 House and Senate incumbents were spending similar amounts of time in their constituencies, but House members were receiving only two-thirds of the travel subsidy that senators could claim: House members were permitted 4 round trips as opposed to 6 for senators. With the same level of travel subsidy (12 round trips), senators were spending about 35 days per session in their states whereas congressmen were spending 50 days per session in their districts (1969–1970).

Why are House members so much more attentive to their constituencies than senators? Again, the explanation seems to rest in the nature of the two-year congressional term, the size of the constituencies, and the extent to which personal contact serves the incumbent's best interests. The longer term of senators and the larger size of their constituencies may make personal contact less effective and efficient. In addition, it is harder to worry about an election that is six years away than one that occurs every two years. One manifestation of this longer time perspective on the part of senators is the appearance of an electoral cycle in attention to the state. As Fenno notes, "senators up for reelection are most active, and recently elected senators seem to engage in more electorally related activity than senators in the middle of their term" (Fenno, 1982, p. 33). This pattern is also evident in the differences in time spent in the state between all senators and those running for reelection: the latter tend to spend greater amounts of time, though the differences are rather slight in most instances (Fig. 5). Personal contact also may better serve the interests of representatives than senators because, for the latter, even the most extensive personal contact with voters may fail to reach a significant proportion of the electorate. For these reasons, then, it might be expected that senators would devote less time to the personal cultivation of their constituencies than representatives. In conclusion, there is strong evidence of aggregate changes in the attentiveness of House and Senate incumbents. These changes appear to be the result of the increases in the travel allowance in both House and Senate and the replacement of less attentive House members by more attentive ones in recent Congresses.

Figure 5.
Mean Number of Days Spent in the State by All Senators and Those Running for Reelection: 1959—1980

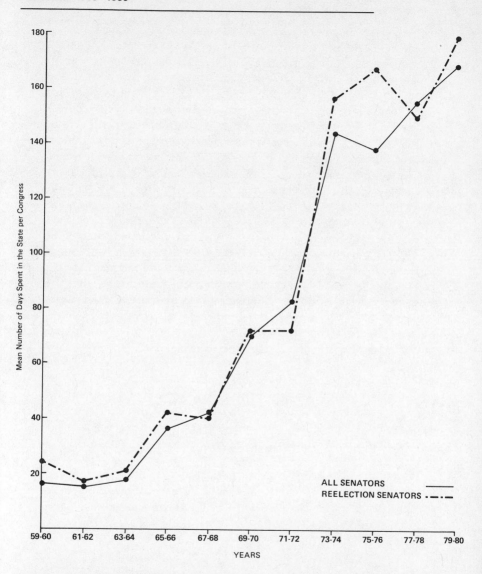

Source: Travel vouchers filed with the secretary of the Senate.

: 4 :

Institutional Incentives for Home-Style Change

Changes in attention to constituency have occurred because they satisfy a variety of needs on the part of members—specifically, the need to maintain electoral safety, provide services to constituents, and to gain a degree of freedom to pursue policy interests or positions of power in Congress. These provided the motivations for the adoption of more attentive home styles, a major element of which is direct and indirect contact with constituents. These contacts provide the chemistry that keeps a successful electoral coalition intact and builds constituents' trust. Every congressman and senator probably knows of at least one colleague who experienced defeat for failing to keep the home "fences mended." Such lessons may not be widespread, but their mere existence undoubtedly has the effect on many incumbents of reinforcing the importance of spending time with constituents.

Legislator-constituent contact frequently occurs as incumbents seek to resolve or redress constituents' grievances. Sometimes these problems involve the operations of the federal bureaucracy; in these cases, the incumbent performs the role of legislative ombudsman. At other times, constituents contact their legislators to receive information or to express opinions. Most of these communications are routine and do not require the personal attention or involvement of the incumbent since the office staff normally can handle them. Nevertheless, incumbents respond to constituents' inquiries as if they were personally involved in resolving these problems. Newsletters often point to the personal intercession of the member in resolving relatively minor problems of constituents. Responses to inquiries carry the member's name in a smearable ink (to impress the truly skeptical), although few incumbents probably read or sign them. In this way, senators and congressmen promote the image that they are personally involved in serving their constituents. The key word here is *personally*. That is, members do help their constituents, but their personal involvement in such services is often exaggerated. They may not like the "disguise," but they may have little choice because the maintenance of an attentive home style requires the persistence of images that reflect a personal involvement in constituency affairs, no matter how impractical or unrealistic those images may be.

Since actions speak louder than words, personal presence in the constituency serves as irrefutable evidence of the legislator's personal attention to constituents. From the perspective of the constituent, members who stay away from their districts or states create the impression of trying to avoid embarrassment, questions, or political attack since "only the guilty have anything to fear." Conversely, those who appear regularly in front of their constituents demonstrate that they have little to fear, or else they would not take the political risks associated with frequent appearances. Further, frequent stays in the district or state generate opportunities for explaining one's Washington activities to constituents. Explanations enhance trust and therefore provide incumbents with a measure of freedom from their constituents to pursue other goals.

It is advantageous to members to spend as much time as possible both in Washington and at home. The time they spend in Washington can be used both to promote their reelection and to pursue personal goals. The time they spend at home can be used to engage in activities that will help them gain voter support so that they can achieve their more personal political goals. There are strong incentives to engage in both, but at the same time the desire to do so presents an allocative dilemma.

The job of congressman requires that some things be done in Washington and others be done in the district. At the least, legislation is passed in one place and elections occur in the other. The allocative problem, therefore, comes with the job. And this built-in strain between the need to attend to district business affects the work of each individual and the work product of the institution. The strain is both omnipresent and severe. Members give up the job because of it. Congressional reforms are advocated to alleviate it. (Fenno, 1978, p. 33)

There are at least two obstacles to the member's ability to exploit both Washington and home activities: costs in terms of time and money. The decision on the allocation of time is a zero-sum proposition: time spent at home cannot be spent in Washington activities, and vice versa. Speaking of House members, Fenno remarks: "Time is a House member's scarcest and most precious political resource. If there is an exemplary congressional complaint, surely 'there isn't enough time' must be it. In deciding how to spend his time, in Washington, in the district and, for our purposes, between Washington and the district, a member confronts his most difficult allocative dilemma" (ibid., p. 34).

This observation is equally applicable to all members of Congress. Therefore the necessity of choosing one arena over the other is a serious impediment to the efficient exploitation of the opportunities offered by each.

A second obstacle to the efficient exploitation of the opportunities offered in each setting is the financial burden associated with constituency activities. Before the consolidation of office resources, ceilings were placed on the subsidies provided by the government for different home activities. Even if a member's schedule could be juggled to permit the allocation of more time to home activities, the number of reimbursed trips was limited. Unless a member was willing to subsidize such travel personally or could find another source of funding (such as lobbying organizations), there was an effective limit on the time that could be spent at home. After the consolidation of allowances, the member was still faced with the same allocative problem as existed with regard to time; money spent for travel could not be spent for other things such as additional mailings.

While it would be optimal for senators and representatives to take full advantage of the opportunities offered by both Washington and home activities, the costs involved limit their ability to do so. If members could reduce the costs of engaging in home activities, there would be increased incentives to allocate more resources to them. Institutional changes are one means of doing this. As Mayhew (1974a) notes, institutional arrangements in Congress are designed for electoral benefit. In the same way, the institution can promote home-style activities by reducing the costs to members. Three methods of reducing these costs, and thereby increasing the incentives to perform such activities, are cost subsidization, cost shifting, and conflict reduction through legislative scheduling.

TYPES OF INSTITUTIONAL INCENTIVES

As Congress accommodated to the needs of its members to maintain contact with their constituents, it facilitated changes in attention by reducing the direct costs associated with it. Some of this cost reduction was accomplished by increasing the subsidies for various constituency activities and expanding the perquisites available for maintaining contact with constituents. Other costs were made more transferrable. I have already noted the ability of a member's staff to absorb much of the routine work associated with casework; hence members could expand their services to the constituency without feeling the full brunt of the increased contact with constituents.

There have also been efforts to reduce the competition for a member's time that is created by legislative (Washington) demands and those of the constituency. For instance, the legislative schedule has been structured by confining legislative business to certain days (Tuesday to Thursday) to facilitate contact with constituents. Thus the perquisites and the legislative schedule have been altered to promote attentive home styles. By manipulating the legislative schedule and reducing the costs associated with attention to the constituency, Congress altered the opportunity structure and facilitated the conversion of members to higher levels of attention.

Subsidization

The most direct way in which institutional incentives for attention can be provided is through direct subsidies for these activities. Many such services are subsidized through legislatively authorized allowances (Table 19). Prior to recent reforms in Congress, separate allowances were maintained for such expenses as telephones and telegrams, postage and special delivery, and staff and travel. Since unused portions of these allowances were returned to the Treasury,

Table 19
Increases in House Perquisites, 1945–1975[a]

Specific Allowance	1945–1960	1961–1975
Clerk-hire (number of staff)	5 (1945)	9 (1961)
	6 (1949)	10 (1964)
	7 (1954)	11 (1966)
	8 (1955)	12 (1969)
		15 (1971)
		16 (1972)
		18 (1975)
Postage (dollars per session for airmail and special delivery)	$ 90 (1945)	$500 (1963)
	125 (1952)	700 (1968)
	200 (1954)	910 (1971)
	300 (1957)	1140 (1974)
	400 (1959)	
Telephone and telegraph (units)	40,000 (1959)	45,000 (1962)
		50,000 (1963)
		70,000 (1967)
		80,000 (1970)
		100,000 (1973)
		125,000 (1975)
Travel allowance (round trips per session)		2 (1963)
		4 (1965)
		12 (1967)
		18 (1973)
		26 (1975)

Source: Committee on House Administration.

a. These separate allowances were consolidated into the official expense allowance in 1978.

there were strong incentives for members to take full advantage of them.[1]

The franking privilege is just one example of a subsidy that can serve as a direct incentive for increasing levels of contact with the constituency.[2] American households are bombarded at regular intervals with an assortment of mail that bears the signature of a member of Congress in lieu of postage. The ease with which such mail can be addressed, the number of constituents who can be reached, and the absence of direct costs to members for exercising this privilege make mass mailings a useful mechanism for maintaining contact. Further, there is an economy-of-scale incentive for expanding this type of service if subsidies are increased. Once such a service is established, the direct marginal cost to the member of expanding it is small. Mass mailings, for instance, can be distributed to a broader group without the member incurring any additional personal costs.

The restrictions placed on the use of the congressional frank are quite narrow and specific: members are prohibited from using it for mailings that are designed to solicit political support. However, even mailings falling into the prohibited category are subsidized through the postage allowance. While this allowance is considerably smaller and less extensive than the frank, each office receives an allowance for official mail that is ineligible for franking.

Another example of direct subsidization is the provision of allowances to defray the monetary costs of traveling to the district or state. The institution of this allowance in the Senate in 1958 and in the House in 1963 meant that these expenses no longer had to be covered out-of-pocket or by friendly lobbies. I view the expansion of subsidies for mailings, travel, and staff as a critical factor in facilitating changes in the way in which members relate to their constituencies.

In Table 19 the post–World War II increases in four categories of House office expenses are enumerated. It is clear that most of the increases in these categories occur after 1960. All of the increases in the travel allotment occur in the 1960s and 1970s, and the clerk-hire allowance doubled between 1961 and 1975. This pattern of post-1960 increases in office perquisites can also be found in the growth of Senate allowances. For example, the Senate postage allowance rose by $150 between 1956 and 1960, but by about $500 between 1961 and 1966; between 1966 and its consolidation with other expenses in 1973, it was increased by about 50 percent. The increases in these allowances provided the resources necessary for maintaining an attentive home style and expanding constituent-legislator contact. Further, increases in these allowances reduced the costs associated with attention to the constituency and therefore increased the incentives to exploit these opportunities. The comments of one House incumbent interviewed by Fenno suggest the importance of travel subsidies in generating attention to district affairs. "In the early years, I didn't make many trips home. It was simply a matter of money . . . I come home more now. I get a bigger travel allowance and I get asked to speak more. I never pay any of my own money to come home. I can't" (Fenno, 1978, pp. 52–53).

Cost Shifting

Increases in the subsidies for staff provide an example of a more indirect method of reducing the costs attached to constituency attention—cost shifting. As I noted earlier, one of the inherent limitations on the ability to take advantage of opportunities to engage in attention to the constituency is that a member's time is finite. If there were some way of shifting the personal costs of services to someone else, a member would have more time to engage in these activities. The use of staff for constituency services helps members to shift the burden of such activities without reducing the level of service to the constituent.

Staff are at the center of the "small business" operations that characterize House and Senate offices.[3] These offices have been termed "member enterprises" because of the multiplicity of activities they perform to further the member's interests, especially district interests. "With extensive staff resources, member-enterprises can actively seek out district-related aspects of policy proposals or of programs already in operation. They can tack on amendments with special district appeal. They can articulate whatever differential district advantages there may be in a particular program" (Salisbury and Shepsle, 1981, p. 571). Senators and representatives have long recognized the value of staff in serving as their surrogates; this recognition is evident in the efforts of members to increase the level of travel to the constituency permitted to their staffs. For instance, Senator Mark Hatfield (R-Oregon) echoed the sentiment of most senators when he urged the passage of legislation that would reimburse staff for travel within the home state. "What staff members are able to do in all states when they assist constituents in this manner is to help cut red tape facing everyone dealing with government. In addition, better communication is achieved. Eyeball-to-eyeball contact is what should be encouraged. This bill will assist in enabling our staffs to better serve our constituents" (U.S. Congress, 1972, p. 7).

Since office staff serve a number of functions, both legislative and related to the constituency, one cannot attribute the growth in staff entirely to increases in the demands of and services to the constituency.

The staff explosion came about for a variety of reasons: a desire for congressional independence from the executive branch; the increasing volume and complexity of legislative issues faced by Congress; the decline of the congressional seniority system; a growing sense that the minority party in Congress should get fairer treatment; competition among committees and their members; election of more activist members; greater demands exerted by special interests; and an increase in mail and demands for services by constituents. (Congressional Quarterly, 1983, p. 125)

Whatever the reason behind the expansion of office staff in Congress, the increase has helped members to reduce the costs of attention to the constituency by shifting some of the burdens of it to staff members.

Scheduling

Another method of reducing the costs attached to attention is to structure the legislative schedule to allow members to spend time in their districts and states without detracting from their Washington responsibilities. As a general rule, time spent in the district or state is time well spent for incumbents because it contributes to their visibility and provides valuable opportunities to focus attention on activities that create a favorable image in their constituents' minds. By structuring the legislative schedule so that members can spend time with their constituents without jeopardizing legislative interests or responsibilities, Congress has helped to reduce the costs of attention. In the process, increased attention to constituency affairs has been encouraged.

There are several ways in which the legislative schedule in the House and the Senate has been structured to facilitate the adoption of attentive home styles. Congress, especially the House, is infamous for its Tuesday-to-Thursday schedule of legislative business. This truncated schedule enables House members to spend weekends in their districts (a good time for maximizing contact with constituents), without missing any legislative business. The House has also institutionalized periods for travel in the constituency by setting aside blocks of time in the legislative schedule. There is generally little relationship between voting participation in Washington and time spent in the district or state, since most legislative business is scheduled to minimize conflicts with travel to the constituency. Few members need to worry about their absenteeism becoming a campaign issue because incumbents rarely miss a vote unless they really want to avoid taking a position on an issue.

In the Senate, the scheduling of most business is, by definition, acceptable to all, since it is conducted under unanimous consent agreements. These agreements are negotiated between the minority and majority party leaders and must receive the unanimous approval of the Senate; once approved, they serve as the schedule of business.[4] As a result, scheduling decisions in the Senate are as accommodative to their members as are those in the House. Any decision that requires unanimous consent ensures that none are disadvantaged, unless they agree to be disadvantaged (Buchanan and Tullock, 1967).

It is interesting to note that the use of unanimous consent agreements in the Senate increased at the same time as institutional changes encouraging increased attention were occurring among senators: use of unanimous consent agreements (per days in session) increased from 14 percent in 1959 to 37 percent in 1975 (Oleszek, 1978, Table 6–2, p. 144). Such accommodations could have helped to facilitate changes in the attentiveness of senators by reducing the conflicts between legislative business in Washington and time spent at home.

Perhaps the most obvious way in which Congress structures the legislative schedule to reduce the costs of attention to the constituency is through the proliferation of recess periods. Congress normally conducts no legislative business during recess periods; hence members need not worry about forsaking their legislative responsibilities while spending time with their constituents. Some recess and holiday periods are even dictated by statute.[5] For example, the Legislative

Reorganization Act of 1970 specified that, during the first session, Congress was to adjourn from the thirtieth day before to the second day following Labor Day. In essence, this legislation set aside the entire month of August for a congressional recess period. Although the establishment of the August recess had a significant effect on the overall number of recess days allocated, the rise in recess days began even earlier. As Figure 6 reveals, the number of days on which the House and Senate were in recess began to rise in the mid-1960s; this increase coincides with the growth in other perquisites that facilitated constituent-legislator contact.[6]

THE IMPACT OF INSTITUTIONAL INCENTIVES

If institutional changes can provide an impetus for long-term changes in members' home styles, it should be possible with the time spent measure to detect aggregate changes in the number of days members spend at home. That is, government subsidization and legislative scheduling should affect the amount of time that representatives and senators spend in their districts or state monthly. There are at least two reasons for pursuing this question of change in style further through the use of a sophisticated time-series design and analysis. First, I have argued that the increases in perquisites in general, and travel allowances in particular, exerted a permanent change in home style. To demonstrate this effect, it is necessary to show that each successive increase in the travel allowance had lasting effects on attentiveness. Second, since my concern has been with individual congresses, I have no evidence that the effects of the travel allowance shaped the daily behavior of congressmen and senators. It is quite possible that increases in the travel allowance meant only that incumbents could spend more time in their constituencies near election time. The concentration of increases in attentiveness in this manner could be attributed to electoral cycles but would provide little evidence of change in home style. The time-series design permits one to isolate the effects of cycles, such as those associated with elections, and to control for these effects in estimating the causal impact of increased travel allowances and legislative scheduling on the time members spend monthly in the district or state.

The dependent variable in this part of the study is the mean number of days per month that representatives and senators spend in the district or state. The monthly travel of each chamber will be analyzed separately. The span of the analysis in the Senate is from

Figure 6.
Trends in House and Senate Recess Periods: 1958—1980

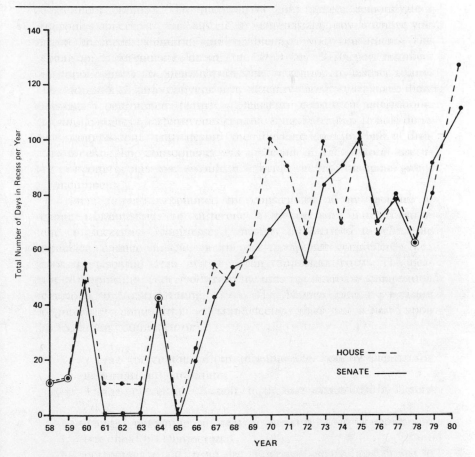

Source: Congressional Directory, 1981, pp. 368—75.

1958 through 1980, and in the House it is from 1963 through 1980. I will examine two institutional changes that I feel have increased the incentives for attention to the constituency: cost subsidization and legislative scheduling.

As Figure 7 shows, the amount of time members spend monthly in their districts and states over the course of this study has increased dramatically. There are two general features of this graph that warrant notice. First, the fluctuations in House and Senate attention appear to coincide. Second, House incumbents appear to be more attentive to their constituencies than senators, and the differences appear to be increasing. (I will return to these observations in the concluding sections of chaps. 4 and 5.) As I noted in chapter 3 (Table 12), travel allowances grew steadily in both chambers after their enactment. I hypothesize that each of these increases had a significant and permanent effect on the amount of time members spend in their districts and states. That is, an increase in the travel allowance should have produced a significant increase in the mean number of days per month that representatives and senators spent at home over the course of the study. The impact of each increase on time spent is examined.

The indicator of scheduling change is the number of recess days per month in each chamber. If recess days are scheduled to allow members to avoid missing important legislative business while they are in their constituencies, then recesses should also increase the number of days per month members spend there. Unlike an increase in travel allowances, however, an individual recess period should not have a long-term or permanent effect in the time spent at home. Instead, recesses should produce impulses in travel during the month in which they occur: immediate and temporary shifts in attention to the constituency.

End of session (EOS) is the final independent variable considered in the analysis. It is included so that the fact that members do not spend as much time in the district or state during certain periods may be taken into consideration. The times between sessions (December and January) and between Congresses (November, December, and January) are not prime periods for attention to constituency (Parker, 1980b). First, they encompass a traditional family holiday, which is a

Figure 7.
Mean Number of Days per Month Spent by Senate and House Incumbents in Their Constituencies: 1959–1980

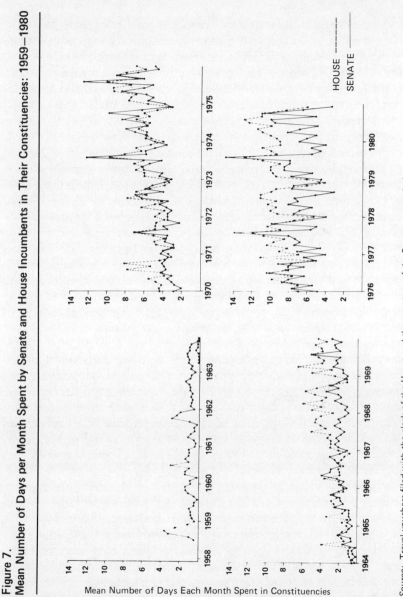

Source: Travel vouchers filed with the clerk of the House and the secretary of the Senate, respectively.

less advantageous time for contacting constituents. Second, no legislative business is conducted during these times, and therefore, there are no Washington activities to explain to constituents. It is expected that the end of session variable will diminish time spent in the constituency (negative relationship). Like recesses, end of session will have a temporary impact.

The questions posed here regarding changes in time spent in the constituency lend themselves to an interrupted time-series analysis. "Interrupted time-series analysis requires knowing the specific point in the series when a treatment occurs. The purpose of the analysis is to infer whether the treatment had an impact. If it did, then we would expect the observations after treatment to be different from those before it. That is, the series should show signs of an interruption at an expected point in time" (Cook and Campbell, 1979, p. 207). There are problems associated with this type of analysis. First, ordinary least squares (OLS) regression cannot be used to determine the impact of the independent variables. The use of time-series data generally violates the assumption of no autocorrelation. Using OLS regression in this case results in unbiased estimates but biased tests of significance. The tendency is for the t-test to overestimate the significance of the interventions.

To minimize this problem, I use the Box-Jenkins ARIMA modeling technique to estimate the effects of the independent variables. This method permits the unbiased estimation of the significance of the coefficients by modeling the systematic component of the error term (the noise model) as part of the estimating equation. (See Box and Jenkins, 1976; McCleary and Hay, 1980; McCain and McCleary, 1979; Hibbs, 1974 and 1977, for a further explanation of this method.)

A second problem associated with time-series analysis is the lack of a sufficient number of data points. The n-sizes for this analysis (n = 216 in the House and n = 276 in the Senate) should be sufficient to undertake the analysis. There are only two points at which the lack of a sufficient number of observations could present a problem. In considering the first and last increases in the travel allowance in the House, there may not be enough time points to estimate the significance of the interventions adequately. If this were the case, there would be a tendency to underestimate the impact of these interventions, and caution should therefore be used in interpreting these effects.

A zero-order transfer function model is chosen to represent the increases in allowances, indicating that I expect them to have an immediate and permanent impact on the time spent.[7] One time series is included for each increase in each chamber. These take the form of a step function, coded 0 in each month before the intervention (increase in the travel allowance) and 1 in each month after the intervention. In specific, each series is coded 1 in the first full month in which the new travel allowance was operative. A zero-order transfer model produces one coefficient (W_0) that is interpreted like an unstandardized regression coefficient. There will be 5 series of this type in the analysis of the House data (one for each allowance increase) and 3 series in the Senate. The question addressed is whether increasing the travel allowances had a significant, permanent impact on the amount of time members spent in their districts and states.

The end-of-session and recess variables are expected to have an immediate, temporary impact on time spent. The end-of-session series is coded 1 in December and January between sessions, 1 in November, December, and January between Congresses, and 0 for all other months. The recess series is a continuous series, and the nature of its transfer function model can be determined from an examination of the cross-correlation function (CCF, between series correlation) between the prewhitened recess and prewhitened time-spent series. Prewhitened series are those where adjustments have been made to take into account existing autocorrelation. By prewhitening a time series prior to analysis, the effects of within-series correlation (autocorrelation in the causor series—recesses) can be removed from the cross-correlation function. Both series are prewhitened by the noise model (which identifies the systematic part of the stochastic component) for the recess series.

It is expected that recesses will have an abrupt, temporary impact that will occur immediately (i.e., there will be no lag in its effect). In addition, it will be possible to determine empirically the direction of causation from the cross-correlation function. That is, I hypothesize that recesses "caused" increases in time spent; alternatively, causation could run in the opposite direction—increases in the time spent led to increases in recess days. The causal nature of the relationship can be determined by the appearance of significant "spikes" (significant correlations between causal and dependent series at different lags) in the cross-correlations (see McCleary and Hay, 1980, chap. 5; Box and Jenkins, 1976, chaps. 10 and 11). If significant spikes appear in the negative portion of the CCF, time spent leads to recess days. In the positive portion they indicate that changes in recesses lead to changes in time spent.

Normally, the individual effects of specific variables are estimated within the same equation. This could not be accomplished in the present analysis because of program limitations on the number of parameters capable of being estimated. For this reason, two models have been used to estimate the effects of increases in travel allowances (interventions), end-of-session periods, and number of recess days in increasing attention: one to estimate the effects of travel allowance increases and end-of-session periods, and the other to estimate the influence of recess periods. I do not expect that the use of two equations rather than one for estimating the effects of these three variables produces a misspecification of the nature of the causal relationships in each equation since there are no significant and recognizable patterns in the residuals to the equations. Separate model equations are estimated for Senate and House attention, and comparisons of the influence of the individual variables are made across institutions.

Effects of Subsidization

The first question addressed is whether subsidization in the form of increased travel allowances leads to increased time spent in the district or state.

In the House two models were tested; model 1 contains only the series representing increases in the travel allowance (Table 12). Applying a one-tailed test of significance (critical t = 1.6), three of the five coefficients attain significance. The first increase in the travel allowance in 1965 and the last in 1978 do not appear to have a significant impact on the time spent by House members in their districts. However, caution should be used in accepting this conclusion since, as was mentioned, there may not be a sufficient number of data points to estimate the equilibrium level of the preintervention period in 1965 and the postintervention period in 1978.

Paring the model to the three significant interventions and adding the end-of-session variable, one finds that the increases in 1973 (I3) and 1978 (I5) had a significant impact (alpha≤.05) on the number of days per month representatives spent in their districts (Table 20); the eight-trip increase in allowances in 1967 (I2) just fails to meet the .05 significance level (.09>alpha>.05). The 1967 increase of 12 trips produced a .93-day increase per month, or an increase of 11 days per year in the amount of time representatives spent in their districts. The next two increases (I3 and I4) each increased time spent by an additional 14 days per year. The end-of-session variable is significant beyond the .05 level and in the anticipated direction. This relationship indicates that representatives spend less time in their districts during the periods falling between the end of one session of Congress and the beginning of the next. The residuals for House model 2 are white noise (random error) with a Q statistic that is significant only between the .50 and .25 levels.[8] A white noise process consists entirely of random shocks (errors) that are uncorrelated with each other, therefore increasing confidence that the observed relationships are not being distorted by autocorrelation.

The comparable model for the Senate series indicates that all three increases in the travel allowance (Table 20) are significant at or beyond the .05 level. The first increase in 1965 (I1) produced a 14-day increase in time spent per year by senators; the second (I2) increased time spent by an additional 10 days per year; and the last increase (I3) in 1973 increased time spent by an additional 19 days. The end-of-session variable operates in much the same way as in the House, decreasing travel between Congresses and sessions.

The Q statistic for model 2 indicates that I have been unable to reduce the residuals for this model to purely white noise (.05>alpha>.02). However, no significant spikes appear in the residual ACF or PACF, the existence of which would indicate an inappropriate model. Further, several other models, including a logged time-spent series, also failed to reduce the series to white noise. The model selected for presentation had the smallest residual mean square (error) and comes the closest of all the models examined to reducing the residuals to white noise. The complexity of the seasonal component of the noise model appears to reflect the staggering of election terms in the Senate. Research suggests that senators devote the most time to attention to the constituency in the last four years of their terms

Table 20
Interventions and Time Spent

	Model 1 $Y_t = W_0 I1 + W_0 I2 + W_0 I3 + W_0 I4 + W_0 I5 + noise$	Model 2 $Y_t = W_0 I2 + W_0 I3 + W_0 I4 + EOS + noise$
House		
Interventions		
I1–2 trips increase (1965)	$W_0 = -.2868$ (t=-.5)	
I2–8 trips increase (1967)	$W_0 = 1.031$ (t=1.9)	$W_0 = .9312$ (t=1.3)
I3–6 trips increase (1973)	$W_0 = .9550$ (t=1.7)	$W_0 = 1.2413$ (t=1.8)
I4–8 trips increase (1975)	$W_0 = 1.2028$ (t=2.2)	$W_0 = 1.1832$ (t=1.6)
I5–6 trips increase (1978)	$W_0 = -.0346$ (t=-.1)	
End of session (EOS)		$W_0 = -1.7917$ (t=-8.0)
(Critical t, one tailed = 1.60)		
Noise model	ARIMA (011) (200)$_{12}$ $\Theta_1 = .898$ (t=29.3) $\Phi_{12} = .232$ (t=3.3) $\Phi_{24} = .442$ (t=6.3)	ARIMA (011) (100)$_{12}$ $\Theta_1 = .808$ (t=20.1) $\Phi_{12} = .221$ (t=2.6)
Other information	N=216 RMS=1.548 Q=50.1 (df=23)	N=216 RMS=1.362 Q=28.2 (df=24)

	Model 1 $Y_t = W_0 I1 + W_0 I2 + W_0 I3 + \text{noise}$	Model 2 $Y_t = W_0 I1 + W_0 I2 + W_0 I3 + EOS + \text{noise}$
Senate		
Interventions		
I1–4 trips increase (1965)	$W_0 = 1.1991$ (t=2.8)	$W_0 = 1.1910$ (t=2.8)
I2–6 trips increase (1969)	$W_0 = .8118$ (t=1.7)	$W_0 = .8112$ (t=1.8)
I3–8 trips increase (1973)	$W_0 = 1.6053$ (t=3.9)	$W_0 = 1.6166$ (t=3.9)
End of session (EOS)		$W_0 = -1.3055$ (t=-1.6)
(Critical t, one tailed = 1.60)		
Noise model	ARIMA (012) (200)$_{12}$ (100)$_{48}$	ARIMA (012) (200)$_{12}$ (100)$_{48}$
	$\Theta_1 = .733$ (t=12)	$\Theta_1 = .732$ (t=12)
	$\Theta_2 = .223$ (t=3.5)	$\Theta_2 = .224$ (t=3.5)
	$\Phi_{12} = .170$ (t=2.8)	$\Phi_{12} = .152$ (t=2.5)
	$\Phi_{24} = .395$ (t=5.5)	$\Phi_{24} = .385$ (t=5.4)
	$\Phi_{48} = .594$ (t=7.5)	$\Phi_{48} = .590$ (t=7.5)
	N=276	N=276
	RMS=1.247	RMS=1.239
	Q=35.2 (df=21)	Q=35 (df=21)
Other information		

(Taggart and Durant, 1984). Coupled with the staggered term, this could lead to the complexity of the seasonal component of the noise model.

Effects of Scheduling

The transfer functions for the House and Senate recess series are the same for both chambers. (See Appendix for the CCFs of the prewhitened recess series and the prewhitened time-spent series.) In each case, recesses have an immediate impact, significantly increasing time spent in the same month as the recess (Table 21). Further, in the month following the recess, time spent appears to decline by an equivalent amount. The CCFs for each chamber also indicate that the hypothesized direction of causation holds: recesses lead to increased time spent rather than vice versa (See Appendix).

In the models containing the House and Senate recess series, the residuals are reduced to white noise (Table 21). Once again, the noise model for the Senate series contains a complex seasonal component. In both cases, there are no significant spikes in the ACF or PACF for the residuals. The prewhitening models for the recesses were determined from a univariate analysis; all the parameters in these prewhitening models are significant at the .05 level or beyond. Since the cross-correlation functions for the prewhitened recess series and the model residuals for both the House and Senate have no significant spikes, I have identified an adequate model (transfer function).

While the effects of recesses are short lived in terms of inducing greater attention to district or state, the growth in the number of days during the year when the House and the Senate are in recess (Fig. 6) suggests a more enduring impact. The increases in recess days have increased the opportunities for members to travel to their districts and states without fear of neglecting legislative duties. Briefly put, a day here and there added to the amount of time that senators and congressmen could spend in their constituencies eventually become additional weeks of recess. Thus, despite its immediate effect, the growth in recess days means that the legislative schedule has been structured to promote more opportunities for contact with the constituency. In this way, recesses have had a long-term impact on changes in the attentiveness of congressmen and senators.

Table 21
Impact of Recesses on Time Spent

HOUSE

	Parameter (t-value)
Transfer function model $\nabla Y_t = (W_0 - W_1 B)X_t + \text{noise}$	$W_0 = .0947$ (t=7.5) $W_1 = .1172$ (t=11.3)
Noise model ARIMA (001) (100)$_{48}$	$\Theta_1 = .653$ (t=11.3) $\Phi_{48} = .370$ (t=4.5)
Prewhitening model (recess) ARIMA (001) (200)$_{12}$	$\bar{X} = 6.441$ $\Phi_1 = .1730$ $\Phi_{12} = .2820$ $\Phi_{24} = .4710$
Other information	$N = 216$ $RMS = 1.191$ $Q = 32(\text{df}=24)$

SENATE

	Parameter (t-value)
Transfer function model $\nabla Y_t = (W_0 - W_1 B)X_t + \text{noise}$	$W_0 = .093$ (t=7.5) $W_1 = .097$ (t=7.7)
Noise model ARIMA (011) (200)$_{12}$ (100)$_{48}$	$\Theta_1 = .592$ (t=9.9) $\Theta_2 = .287$ (t=4.7) $\Phi_{12} = .207$ (t=3.4) $\Phi_{24} = .310$ (t=4.5) $\Phi_{48} = .508$ (t=6.4)
Prewhitening model (recess) ARIMA (100) (200)$_{24}$	$\bar{X} = 6.383$ $\Phi_1 = .127$ $\Phi_{24} = .162$ $\Phi_{48} = .656$
Other information	$N = 276$ $RMS = 1.031$ $Q = 18.4$ (df=21)

CONCLUSIONS

The preponderance of evidence from this analysis indicates that increases in travel allowances have had a significant and permanent impact on the home style of members (as measured by time spent in the state or district). This suggests that reductions in the costs of attention brought about by subsidization produced changes in the way that members relate to their constituents by increasing the incentives for greater attentiveness. The second important finding is that legislative scheduling also significantly influenced the amount of time members spent at home. These two findings support the hypothesis that institutional changes in the opportunity structure of Congress have produced significant changes in home style.

It is also important to note that the changes in behavior became permanent features of representational styles. Each increase in subsidized travel in the Senate and House brought about further increases in time spent beyond the level that had already been established. There are several possible explanations why such behavior changes should become permanent. First, most members view constituency service as an important function of their role and readily accept the responsibilities that go with the job. For instance, the survey of House members conducted by the Obey Commission in 1977 found that 79 percent of those interviewed felt that service to the district was an essential representational obligation (U.S. Congress, 1977). A second factor may well be that members find such service intrinsically rewarding. They have the satisfaction of seeing an immediate and direct effect of their actions. In fulfilling their legislative responsibilities, it is more difficult for them to have a direct impact since each member is only one of many people who influence the passage of major legislation. Constituency service, however, is one area where a member can exercise a great deal of influence.

Perhaps the most important factor that could motivate legislators to adopt more attentive styles is their perception of the potential payoffs from such a change. They perceive that the way in which they relate to their constituencies can affect their chances for reelection. In fact, Fenno points out that members believe this to be a critical factor (Fenno, 1978, p. 210). There is evidence to suggest that this is not merely a matter of false perceptions on the part of members. Examination of voter likes and dislikes about representatives shows that generally constituency service is viewed favorably. In addition, this is one area of performance that challengers cannot claim credit for, and thus an incumbent has a distinct advantage over any opponent (see chap. 5).

Members may also be able to use constituency services to buy leeway from both their constituency and their party. This leaves them free to pursue less proximate goals. As Fenno's (1978) examination of home styles suggests, a member's activities in the home district or state are designed to win the trust of constituents. Such trusting behavior can free members to pursue policies that may not necessarily be supported by constituents. It can also free a member from pressures applied by party leaders since members with a trusting constituency are less dependent on the benefits that can be provided by the party: they maintain their own effective campaign and reelection apparatus. Thus increasing attentiveness may allow members more leeway in pursuing personal goals.

Cultivating the trust of constituents in order to gain greater leeway in their actions in Washington may also allow members to pursue power and other goals within Congress. In the case of both policy and power, however, leeway from the constituency may not be sufficient to attain these goals. The structure of Congress must also be conducive. If, having gained the freedom to pursue less proximate goals, a member finds the institution inhospitable to such pursuits, the additional constituent activities have been for naught. This suggests a potential consequence of increased constituency service—demands for further changes in the institution so that members are able to satisfy other goals. I will discuss this point further in chapter 6.

Scholars have argued that the expansion of office "perks" strengthened the electoral position of incumbents (Mayhew, 1974a; Cover, 1977), but few studies have verified such an electoral effect to perquisite usage (Ferejohn, 1977; Born, 1982). From my perspective, the expansion of perquisites associated with constituency service increased the opportunities for changes in constituency attention; such changes in home style, in turn, promoted the electoral safety of extremely marginal incumbents (i.e., those who represented politically atypical districts and states). Therefore, perquisite usage may have an effect on electoral safety. This can occur because such perquisites are indirectly related to electoral safety vis-à-vis their linkage to home-style changes. That is, the expansion of perquisites facilitated the adoption by atypical congressmen and senators of more attentive home styles, which enhanced electoral safety. Such indirect, nonlin-ear linkages between electoral safety and perquisite increases could account for the inability of congressional scholars to uncover a simple relationship between the two. The expansion of perquisites during this period facilitated the changes in attention to the constitu-ency that I uncovered in chapter 3 and the electoral safety of House and Senate incumbents that I will describe in chapter 5.

: 5 :

Home Style and Electoral Competition

There are a variety of incumbent advantages that could conceivably reduce the competitiveness of House and Senate elections, such as perquisites that could be used to entice voter support (Cover and Brumberg, 1982) and campaign contributions that can provide a financial edge for incumbents that few challengers can surmount (Jacobson, 1980). Incumbents also may derive electoral benefits from their ability to do favors for constituents and to bring federal monies to the district or state (Fiorina, 1977). Another electoral advantage associated with incumbency can be added to this list: the ability to focus the attention of constituents on the member's service to the district or state. This enables incumbents to enhance their popularity in the constituency and their subsequent electoral support. In this chapter, I examine two major questions: the value of attention to the constituency in image building and in generating popularity, and the effects of changes in attentiveness on the decline in competition over time in House and Senate elections.

Attention to the constituency is a valuable electoral resource for incumbents because voters place such a high value on service to the district or state. As a result, constituency service almost always generates favorable attitudes. For this reason, legislators tend to emphasize their service to the district or state in their face-to-face contacts and written communications with constituents. The benefits of personal attention to constituency affairs outweigh the costs since incumbents are able to promote favorable images of their performance in office—images that enhance their popularity among their constituents.

Personal attention can also reduce electoral competition as attentive members expand the size of their voter coalitions through their office-related contacts in the constituency. Changes in personal attention, therefore, can help to explain the decline over time in competition in congressional elections that has been documented by David Mayhew (1974b) and Morris Fiorina (1977). The main beneficiaries of this increased safety have been the electorally marginal. These members may benefit most from changes in attentiveness because such changes are helpful in broadening minimally winning voter coalitions. In the first part of this chapter I describe the linkage between attention to the constituency and incumbent images and popularity. In the second part I examine the extent to which the decline in competition in the House and Senate can be attributed to changes in style on the part of electorally marginal congressmen and senators.

POPULARITY AS AN ELECTORAL ADVANTAGE

There is considerable evidence to suggest that most incumbents are quite popular with their constituents. The performance of members at home and in Washington, for example, normally receives high marks, especially when compared to the far more critical evaluations of Congress (Parker and Davidson, 1979); constituents are far more willing to laud the performance of their congressman than the Congress. Such popularity serves many electoral purposes such as discouraging electoral challenges.

The electoral value of incumbency lies not only in what it provides to the incumbents, but equally as well in how it affects the thinking of potential opponents and their potential supporters. Many incumbents win easily, by wide margins, because they face inexperienced, sometimes reluctant challengers, who lack the financial and organizational backing to mount a serious campaign for Congress. If an incumbent can convince potentially formidable opponents and people who control campaign resources that he is invincible, he is very likely to avoid a serious challenge and so will be invincible—as long as the impression holds. (Jacobson, 1983, p.37)

But why are incumbents so popular? In the following pages, I offer an explanation.

Focusing Attention

The ability to focus constituents' attention on aspects of job performance (e.g., constituency service) or characteristics related to job performance (e.g., experience) that produce favorable impressions of the incumbent's overall performance in office is a major electoral advantage that should not be underestimated. This ability results from the virtual monopoly of legislators over the dissemination of information about themselves, which tends to draw constituents' attention to actions or characteristics that generate positive evaluations of performance in office. The "advertising" and "credit-claiming" activities that incumbents find electorally useful (Mayhew, 1974a), and the home-style behaviors of House members described by Richard Fenno (1978), can be viewed as continuing efforts to focus constituents' attention. This situation persists because constituents rely upon subsidized information in making judgments about the performance of their legislators, especially their representatives. Anthony Downs noted this dilemma in discussing some of the problems inherent in attempting to reduce rationally the costs of becoming informed. "Whenever information is provided to consumers at a low cost either because of mass production or subsidies or both, each consumer gains financially only by sacrificing control over the selection principles behind the information" (Downs, 1957, p. 230).

While the information provided to constituents is not apocryphal, it may be constructed in such a manner as to lead to the conclusion that the incumbent is performing well. This may explain why most citizens see their representative as doing a good or very good job in Washington. Incumbents can be viewed as behaving much like the propagandists that Downs refers to as "persuaders": "they present correct information organized so as to lead to a specific conclusion" (ibid., p. 84). The conclusion that legislators want their constituents to reach is obvious: the incumbent has served the district or state well. If constituents develop a favorable evaluation of the job performance of incumbents, they have good reason to vote for them, especially in House elections.

House elections are low-information contests (Stokes and Miller,

1966) anyway, where constituents lack the detailed information to make specific distinctions between the candidates and their policy orientations. As a consequence, the voting decision is reduced to a vote for or against change. Downs suggests that a similar phenomenon occurs in presidential elections when voters are insufficiently informed to detect differences between the parties and their stands. "When he believes the two parties have identical platforms and current policies, he no longer knows what specific changes will occur if the opposition wins. Therefore he is forced to base his decision upon his attitude towards change in general" (Downs, 1957, p. 44). In congressional contests, the voter is apt to vote against change, that is, to support the incumbent. This kind of decision can be rationally justified: the challenger might or might not do a better job than the incumbent, but constituents have already received information to persuade them that their representative has done a good job in serving the district. Hence they vote to return the incumbent to office because they fear that replacing the incumbent might reduce (or disrupt) the benefits that have accrued to the district and its constituents as a consequence of the incumbents' efforts.

By fostering favorable impressions of their performance, incumbents successfully boost their popularity within the district or state. The performance ratings they receive from constituents are the best predictors of electoral support and a key component in their electoral safety (Parker, 1980b). It might seem tautological to associate popularity with the electoral success of incumbents: successful candidates are, by definition, popular with their constituents, or else they would no longer be incumbents. On the other hand, popularity can be viewed theoretically and conceptually as an intervening mechanism (construct) that translates the behavior of incumbents into increments of electoral support. That is, congressmen and senators can be viewed as acting in ways that promote their popularity among their constituents and, therefore, their electoral safety. This perspective suggests that there is no quid pro quo relationship between constituency service and electoral support; rather, incumbents seek to promote images that maximize their popularity within their constituencies.

Senators are more electorally vulnerable than representatives, in part because of the differences in the visibility of House and Senate elections and in part because of the greater competition in the dissemination of information. Most of what constituents hear about their representatives is carefully constructed by staff to place the congressman's actions in the most favorable light. Unlike congressmen, senators find that their messages must compete with other producers of information (newspapers, radio, television) for the attention of their constituents. The high visibility and credibility of some of these alternative sources of information mean that the interpretations and descriptions that they disseminate are as believable as the messages that senators deliver personally. This could explain why senators make every effort to have their offices manufacture "news" about themselves that will receive media attention: constituents may be more receptive to these messages because the legitimacy of the medium lends credibility to the messages. Since few district newspapers can afford a Washington correspondent, most information about a House member has its genesis in a congressional office. In contrast, senators are less able to focus the attention of their constituents because the actions of the Senate and senators receive higher levels of media exposure. This prevents them from packaging or structuring all of the information that state residents receive about them, and it restricts their ability to exploit this advantage as fully as House incumbents can.

The greater flow of "free information" in Senate elections (Parker, 1981b) makes these contests more susceptible to the effects of national forces. For instance, Warren Kostroski (1973) has noted the growth of idiosyncratic forces in post–World War II Senate elections; senators may be less successful in focusing constituents' attention because of the contaminating effects of these forces. This seems to be a fairly recent phenomenon, perhaps produced by the same forces that have promoted the saliency of senators in the mass media during past decades (Polsby, 1969). Senators find themselves constantly reacting to national policies and events, whereas House members have greater freedom to insulate their images and elections from these same forces.

Senators seem to lack several advantages that benefit the electoral safety of representatives. As I have mentioned, senators find it more difficult to focus the attention of their constituents because of the media attention that their actions attract. While such attention may be essential to their electoral survival, it also has its hazards. "Senators attract national coverage—a must for any potential presidential contender—but a potential disaster for an incumbent who comes out looking bad on the evening news" (Robinson, 1981, p. 91). And the media do not appear to treat senators with the same equanimity as it reserves for representatives; the relationships of senators with their local media are less symbiotic and intimate. In short, senators lose out simply because they cannot be as close to the local press, or their constituents, as House members.

The diminished control of senators over their media visibility could account for their greater electoral insecurity, but the survival rate of House incumbents suggests that media control per se is not a sufficient explanation of the incumbency advantage. Clearly, a decline in electorally marginal congressional districts has occurred despite the fact that incumbents probably maintained greater control over information about themselves in the past then they do today.[1] This suggests that it is the specific ability to generate favorable perceptions of their job performance, rather than mere information control, that accounts for the electoral success of incumbents.

Attentiveness

Attention to the constituency can be viewed as an electoral advantage that falls to incumbents since they are the only ones in a position to take advantage of it. Simply put, actions speak louder than words, and incumbents can boast about their attention to their constituents, whereas challengers can only promise what they would do if elected. Further, since most incumbents are fairly diligent in looking after their constituents, the challengers' promises of maintaining a comparable level of attention, or of increasing it, may not sound very convincing to voters already satisfied with their representative's performance. The mechanism that translates attention to the constituency into electoral support is popularity, which is a central component in electoral success and prolonged safety.

I have suggested that certain areas of job performance generate positive evaluations of incumbents. What aspects, then, can they magnify to their electoral advantage? Attentiveness to the constituency is one, because it is a class of activities that demonstrates that the incumbent is looking after the interests of the district or state.[2] There are three explanations of the benefits attentiveness provides to incumbents: First, it is frequently mentioned as something that constituents like about incumbents (Parker and Davidson, 1979); the frequency with which it is cited indicates that it is very salient to constituents. Second, there is a clear positive valence attached to district attention—rarely is it mentioned as something that constituents dislike about their representative (Fig. 8).[3] Finally, attentiveness is unlikely to be mentioned in evaluations of challengers to House incumbents. If constituents appreciate the attentiveness of representatives, there is no reason to believe that the attentiveness of senators would be valued any less.

But why should attention to the constituency be so important to constituents? Fiorina (1977) suggests that the growth in the federal government and the corresponding dependence of citizens on the federal bureaucracy that oversees the expanding set of programs has created demands by constituents for assistance from their congressman. There is probably an additional reason: there has been a growing feeling on the part of voters that legislators are inattentive to their constituents, and these perceptions of responsiveness were declining at approximately the same time that Fiorina indicates the need for ombudsman services for the constituency were on the rise. This decline is reflected in the dramatic drop in the proportion of the electorate that perceive members of Congress as devoting a good deal of attention to their constituents (Fig. 9).[4] The decline is not merely a product of the eroding trust in government that has transpired since the 1960s (Miller, 1974); it seems to arise from a feeling of ineffectiveness in influencing the mechanisms of government (external efficacy) (Parker, 1981a).

In a sense, attentiveness to the constituency distinguishes the incumbent from other members of Congress, as well as from the challenger, in the eyes of constituents. This is evident in the fact that people who mention attentiveness in rating job performance perceive their representative as devoting more time than other members of Congress to these activities (Parker, 1981a, p. 46). Further, over one-third of the reasons cited by respondents as a basis for believing their congressman is "better than most other congressmen" made reference to attentiveness (U.S. Congress, 1977, p. 820). Therefore, constituents may be unwilling to remove the incumbent because of the fear that a replacement might be as inattentive to their interests as they perceive other members to be.

Figure 8.
Likes and Dislikes About House Incumbents: 1978 and 1980

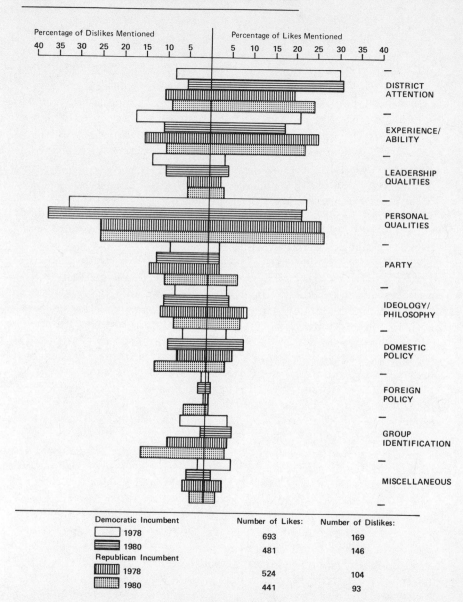

Source: Center for Political Studies, 1978 and 1980.

Figure 9.
Perceptions of the Responsiveness of Members of Congress: 1964—1980

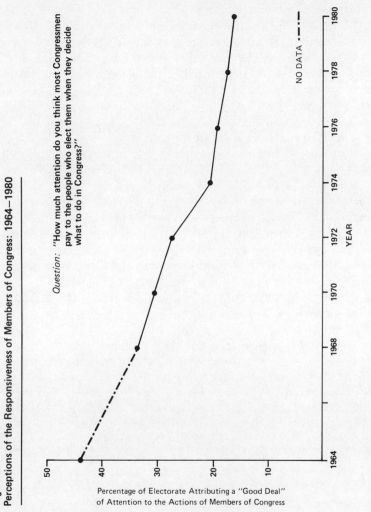

Question: "How much attention do you think most Congressmen pay to the people who elect them when they decide what to do in Congress?"

NO DATA ·—·—·

Percentage of Electorate Attributing a "Good Deal" of Attention to the Actions of Members of Congress

YEAR

Source: Center for Political Studies, 1964—1980.

The Insulation of House Elections

The greater ability of House incumbents to structure constituents' perceptions also enables them to insulate their congressional races better from the vagaries of national forces, such as those commonly associated with presidential elections. Representatives are able to divert constituents' attention away from national events, conditions, and candidates while emphasizing the more positive aspects of their performance, such as their attention to district concerns. This task is made more difficult during presidential elections, which disturb the political tranquility normally exhibited by midterm elections. Presidential elections provide a noisy context for the conduct of congressional races. The expansion of political news, the campaigns of the presidential candidates, and the general excitement that accompanies most presidential elections stimulate the political interest of citizens (Campbell, 1966); midterm congressional elections lack these qualities. In fact, Angus Campbell (ibid.) attributes the normal midterm decline in voter turnout to the lower level of political stimulation that is provided by most congressional contests. Presidential elections systematically heighten political interest, even in congressional races.

For most congressional incumbents, few electoral benefits can be derived from increased political interest during presidential election years because the circumstances that create the surge in interest serve as potential countervailing pressures on the standing decision of the electorate. In presidential elections this standing decision may involve whether to support one party or the other (ibid.), but in congressional elections it has become whether or not to support the incumbent (Ferejohn, 1977). Presidential elections, then, could diminish the ability of House incumbents to focus constituent attention by distracting voters (i.e., monopolizing political news and influencing constituents' perceptions of incumbents). The strong and continuous flow of presidential news also could confound the personalized nature of incumbent images, thereby diminishing the saliency of the incumbent's positive attributes, like district attention. For instance, presidential news and messages and the images of the presidential candidates have the potential to shift constituents' attention away from a congressman's service to the district to partisan, ideological, or issue considerations. In addition, the emphasis on presidential news makes it more difficult for congressional incumbents to promulgate the types of image that enhance their electoral safety. In the same way as presidential news normally crowds out media coverage of Congress (Cornwell, 1959), the media attention given to presidential campaigns results in less attention to congressional candidates and races.

Despite these potentially adverse effects, the images of congressmen are just as resilient during presidential elections as they are during midterm races. As Figure 8 demonstrates, incumbents continue to be perceived in highly personalized terms, their most favorable assets being their experience and attention to the district. Even during presidential elections, policy considerations infrequently influence constituents' evaluations of their congressmen.

The saliency of these images is even more remarkable when one considers the reduction in the channels for conveying such messages. During presidential elections, members have a more difficult time gaining media attention or "space" for promulgating the types of messages that bolster their popularity among their constituents. This reduction in the channels of communication between congressman and constituent does not necessarily lead to greater reliance on other avenues of information. For instance, neither mass mailings nor personal contacts are more important sources of incumbent images in 1980 than in 1978 (not shown). The saliency of these images of representatives probably results from their home styles. These behaviors promote the same message—the incumbent cares about the district—and the repetition that occurs during the campaign prevents other considerations from influencing the perceptions of constituents. If one compares the activities of House members during congressional campaigns (Jones, 1966) and their "normal" home-style behaviors (Fenno, 1978), it is clear that the images and the messages remain largely the same; campaigns only serve to rekindle these images. This is not surprising, since representational and campaign activities are difficult to disentangle. At what point, for instance, in congressman-constituent communications do the attempts of incumbents to inform constituents about their Washington behavior serve an electoral rather than a representational function?

While this discussion suggests that the short-term forces associated with presidential elections and national conditions fail to alter the personalized images of House incumbents, it should not be concluded that national forces have no impact whatsoever on congressional contests. Many of these forces provide advantages and disadvantages that the candidates either mute or capitalize upon in their campaigns. For example, incumbents from the presidents' party may be disadvantaged at the start of the campaign by low levels of presidential popularity, but by the end of the campaign they have either disassociated themselves from the president or reduced the effects of presidential popularity on perceptions of their performance by constituents. As a consequence, congressional contests are insulated from the vagaries of national trends. In addition, national forces can alter the level of competition in congressional elections by influencing the quality of electoral competition (Jacobson and Kernell, 1981).

In sum, national forces can influence congressional races, but House incumbents are normally able to alter or dilute the impact of these short-term forces by focusing constituents' attention on the attributes of the candidates and on local issues. Presidential coattails are weak or nonexistent because congressional elections are insulated from national forces, but their local nature is a product of the actions of House incumbents. If congressional contests are local and personalized affairs, this is due to the successful efforts of House incumbents to keep them that way.

THE IMPACT OF CHANGES IN HOME STYLE ON ELECTORAL COMPETITION

One of the most fascinating features of House and Senate elections is the post-1960s increase in the electoral safety of incumbents. The aggregate increase in electoral safety has been attributed to the disappearance of the types of constituency—marginal ones—that are normally the most susceptible to influence from national swings of opinion (Mayhew, 1974b; Fiorina, 1977). Changes in home styles over time could account for the decline of such competitive areas. Simply put, electorally marginal congressmen and senators could have increased their electoral safety by adopting more attentive home styles; as they became safe, they boosted the overall levels of electoral safety in Congress. Therefore, the analysis in this section examines the ability of marginal incumbents to increase their electoral safety over time by adopting attentive home styles.

The Expansion of Voter Coalitions

Fenno views the processes of building and maintaining electoral support as involving two stages of congressional careers: the expansionist and protectionist stages. In the expansionist stage, members "solidify a primary constituency, a core of strongest supporters who will carry a primary campaign, if necessary, and who will, in any case, provide the backbone for a general election campaign" (Fenno, 1978, p. 172). This stage gives way to the protectionist stage, in which incumbents seek to maintain and stabilize their support. Although Fenno describes these stages as sequential, he notes that some members may find it necessary to lapse into the earlier expansionist stage in response to events.

It is expected that political conditions that create the need to build electoral support would lead to activities associated with an expansionist strategy. For instance, incumbents who are elected from areas with strong opposition party traditions, and who are ideologically divergent from their constituencies, may find it necessary to cultivate state or district voters on a more or less continuous basis. Such members may need to engage in expansionist-stage activities for the duration of their terms in office.

This should not be construed as suggesting that the quantity, or even the quality, of attention to the constituency differs as members progress through the stages of their careers; rather, the focus, diversity, and breadth of that attention may differ depending on whether the aim is to build or to maintain, the electoral coalition. Incumbents in the expansionist stage need to broaden their bases of support by cultivating a wider assortment of groups in the district or state than do incumbents in the protectionist stage, who have the luxury of concentrating their attention on a more limited subset of groups in the constituency. Northern Democratic senators from Republican areas, for example, have an obvious incentive to expand their electoral coalitions. They may direct their constituency activities toward more diverse groups in order to weave majority and minority party voters into successful coalitions. Republican senators from these same areas, on the other hand, can move more rapidly into the protectionist stage and limit their attention to those groups that consistently provide sufficient partisan support to ensure victory. The congressmen and senators who are most inclined to expand their voter coalitions are those from politically atypical areas. Members can be atypical of their constituencies in a number of ways, but the most dramatic seem to relate to partisan loyalties and ideological orientations. Liberals representing conservative constituencies and Democrats elected from Republican areas are two examples of atypical incumbents. It is my contention that changes in home style by House and Senate incumbents from atypical areas helped to improve their reelection margins and augmented aggregate electoral safety during the 1960s and 1970s. These members had the greatest incentive to expand their voter coalitions because their electoral survival depended upon their ability to create coalitions composed of constituents with partisan loyalties to the opposition party or ideological beliefs that would impel loyalty to their opponents. The more politically atypical the area represented, the greater the incumbent's need to expand voter coalitions, and this could have been done by adopting attentive home styles. In the aggregate, these changes produced the decline of competition in the 1960s and 1970s in the House and Senate.

The electoral advantage of House incumbents (Mayhew, 1974b; Fiorina, 1977), and the periodic upsurge in that advantage among northern senators (Mayhew and Cover, 1981), may be due to two related factors: effective exploitation of perquisites, such as travel allowances, and changes in attentiveness to the constituency. Further, the same forces that promoted changes in home styles among atypical representatives can also account for the adoption of more attentive styles among atypical senators. That is, in both cases, incumbents representing constituencies with strong opposition parties and/or differing ideological sentiments found it necessary to develop a means of offsetting normal opposition loyalties among their constituents.

This hypothesized relationship between change in style and increased electoral safety is tested by regressing changes in election margins on changes in the amount of time incumbents spend in their constituencies. The measure of electoral change is the difference in the vote in successive reelections. Similarly, the measure of change in style is the difference in time spent in the district or state during successive Congresses. For example, the effects of changes in attention to the district between the 90th (1967–1968) and 91st (1969–1970) Congresses on the change in electoral vote between 1968 and 1970 will be examined. The functional relationship between change in style and electoral change can be represented in the following manner:

$$Y_t - Y_{t-1} = b(X_t - X_{t-1}) + e_t - e_{t-1}$$

The expression $Y_t - Y_{t-1}$ represents the measurement of electoral change (election vote at time t minus election vote at time $t-1$); $X_t - X_{t-1}$ represents the measurement of change in style in successive elections (time spent in constituency at time t minus time spent in constituency at time $t - 1$); and $e_t - e_{t-1}$ represents the disturbances or error term.

This measure of change in style is modified to capture the interactive effects between change in style and the representation of politically atypical areas, and the impact of these effects on electoral safety in the House and Senate. This is accomplished by introducing additional conditions (multiplicative terms) to the measurement of change in style. The result is an interaction term that reflects the joint influences of change in style and the representation of politically marginal areas on changes in the election margins of Senate and House incumbents between 1964 and 1980. I will explain these modifications in the measure as they enter the analysis of electoral change in the House and Senate.

Finally, it should be noted that there is a methodological advantage to this formulation of change in style: the problem of serial correlation, which normally plagues inferences based upon longitudinal or time-series analysis, is minimized. Serial correlation normally occurs as a by-product of taking measurements on the same units of observation at different points in time. For example, the election margins of individual incumbents can be expected to be correlated, especially the percentages at successive elections. Similarly, levels of attention to constituency during successive Congresses are correlated, since home styles display some permanence over time. Such correlations can introduce biases that could confound the conclusions and interpretations of the relationship between electoral change and change in home style. This formulation of the functional relationship corresponds to a first-differences transformation of these variables (Theil, 1971, pp. 250–54). The first-differences transformation reduces the biasing effects that result from serial correlation. As a consequence, a high degree of confidence is possible in the magnitude and robustness of the reported relationships.

Electoral Safety in the House

One of the most peculiar phenomena in the study of congressional elections is the post-1960 increase in the electoral safety of House incumbents. One of the first pieces of research to document this change was Mayhew's (1974b) study that reported an unusual decline in the number of congressmen with marginal electoral victories during the 1960s and 1970s. He found that those winning reelection with less than 55 percent of the vote were quickly becoming obsolete. Fiorina's conclusion that "the marginal district is going the way of the passenger pigeon" (Fiorina, 1977, p. 8) has been echoed by other scholars (Born, 1979; Alford and Hibbing, 1981).

This decline in electorally marginal congressional districts has stimulated considerable research and has generated a variety of explanations. Some have blamed the disappearance on the growth in the federal bureaucracy (Fiorina, 1977), the lack of qualified congressional challengers (Hinckley, 1980; Jacobson and Kernell, 1981), or the changing behavior of the American electorate (Burnham, 1975; Ferejohn, 1977). To this list of culprits one can add the names of the incumbents themselves: behavior change on their part has turned marginal congressional seats into safe ones. This change involved the adoption of or conversion to more attentive home styles on the part of congressmen from politically atypical areas.

From my perspective, the growth in travel allowances and other perquisites that facilitated legislator-constituent contact and communication during the 1960s and 1970s enabled members representing areas with a contrasting partisan and ideological consensus to expand their voter coalitions. Unable or unwilling to adopt attitudes or identifications more in line with the sentiment of constituents, congressmen from these areas chose instead to try to win over voters with lavish displays of attention. The expansion of the perquisites made such demonstrations possible, and at a minimal cost. Fiorina suggests that just such a process enhanced the survival of Democrats elected from Republican areas in the pro-Democratic landslide in 1964. "In 1964 many of the freshmen were Democrats who had won election in heretofore Republican districts. They can hardly be blamed for assuming that they could not win reelection on policy grounds. They had every incentive to adopt homestyles that emphasized nonprogrammatic constituency service" (Fiorina, 1977, p. 55).

During the late 1950s and throughout the 1960s and 1970s, a large number of congressmen were swept into office from areas where the opposition party was normally quite strong. For example, the 1958, 1964, and 1974 elections brought an unusually large number of Democrats to Congress from traditionally Republican districts. One sign of this was that most of these Democrats actually defeated Republican incumbents rather than winning open seats (a race where there is no incumbent).

Figure 10 displays the trend in the number of congressmen who defeated an incumbent from the opposition party or captured a seat previously held by it between 1954 and 1980. Such switch-seat victories reached abnormal proportions in 1958, 1964, and 1974. In each of these elections, more than 50 House seats changed party control, and large numbers of Democrats captured Republican seats. For instance, in 1958, 49 of the 50 seats that changed party control (switch- and open seats) were won by Democrats. In 1964, 47 of the 57 seats that switched party control were formerly held by Republicans. While Republican congressional candidates also have made inroads into Democratically controlled House districts, many of the switch-seats (especially those outside of the South) won by Republicans probably represent some recapture of losses to Democrats at the previous election. This would certainly explain the increase in the number of switch-seats captured by Republicans following elections where Democrats defeated a large number of Republican incumbents (Fig. 10).

Thus the nature of turnover during this period led to the election of large numbers of House members from areas where the opposition party was strong, if not entrenched. Normally, party organizations serve as the vital core of electoral coalitions; however, members elected from politically atypical areas found it necessary to expand their voter coalitions beyond the narrow confines of their minority-

Figure 10.
Congressional Seats That Changed Political Party Control: 1954–1980

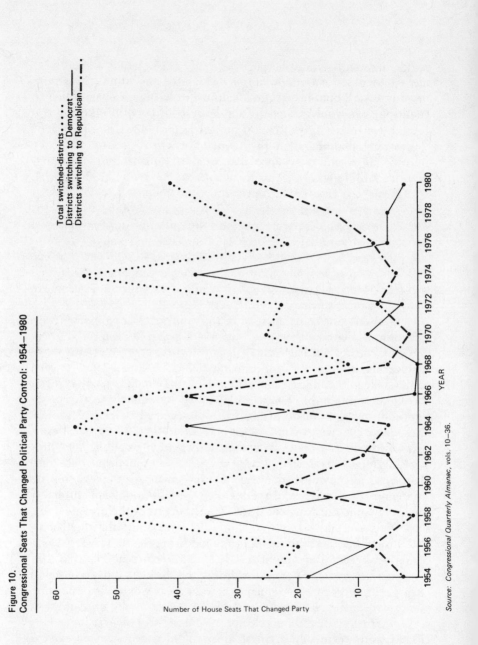

Total switched-districts ·······
Districts switching to Democrat ───
Districts switching to Republican ─·─·

Number of House Seats That Changed Party

YEAR

Source: *Congressional Quarterly Almanac*, vols. 10–36.

party supporters. For these members, the party organization was an ineffective base for building a successful voter coalition. By adopting more attentive home styles, many hoped to fashion a successful voter coalition that would transcend the bounds of party loyalties: a personal following.

Incumbents elected from areas with strong opposition party traditions and loyalties found a way to increase their electoral safety without switching parties or subjugating their political positions to constituents' opinion. The method was quite simple: demonstrate a thorough concern for the district by emphasizing how attentive you are to the needs, demands, and problems of your constituents. The expansion of perquisites during the 1960s and 1970s gave members the opportunities to demonstrate their attention to district affairs. The adoption of and conversion to attentive home styles made these messages a permanent feature of legislator-constituent interactions. In sum, changes in attentiveness enabled these members to hold on to their congressional seats despite their deviance from the bulk of their constituents. The consequence was a decline in the electoral insecurity of congressmen who would be a priori the most marginal group of incumbents.

I have already explained the construction of my measure of change in home style: the difference in the time spent in the constituency in successive Congresses. I modify this variable to reflect the impact of changes in style on the part of atypical congressmen (i.e., those representing areas with a strong opposition party). The measure of atypicality is derived from the index of interparty competition developed by Austin Ranney (1976). The Ranney Index is a measure of interparty competition for state elective offices and is based upon the following computations:

1. average percentage of the popular vote won by Democratic gubernatorial candidates;
2. average percentage of seats in the state senate held by Democrats;
3. average percentage of seats in the state house of representatives held by Democrats;
4. percentage of all terms for governor, senate, and house in which Democrats had control.

There are a number of advantages to using the Ranney Index, the most important being that it is based entirely on competition for state offices. As such, it provides a measure of party competition more removed from national political effects and more sensitive to the long-term partisan traditions within the state than other measures based upon competition for national offices. Thus members from states where their political party has fared poorly during past decades in state electoral contests are assumed to be atypical of the partisan nature of the state. I expect such members to relieve their electoral anxieties by devoting considerable effort to the expansion of their existing coalitions through their attentiveness to district affairs.

States are scored on the Ranney Index in terms of Democratic domination of state offices: the index ranges from 1 for solid Democratic states, to 0 for solid Republican ones. Since I want this measure to reflect political competition for both Democratic and Republican incumbents, I have modified the index to reflect this fact simply by subtracting the Ranney Index score from 1 for every Democratic congressman:

$$(1 - \text{state's score on Ranney Index})$$

Thus low scores on the original Ranney Index (which would reflect Republican domination of the electoral politics within the state) are translated into high scores by my modification of the index for Democratic incumbents. High scores on my modified index reflect one-party domination of state politics by the opposition party, while low scores reflect domination by the incumbent's party. In short, congressmen from states that are electorally safe for their political party receive low values on the transformed index, while those from states dominated by the opposition party receive higher scores. For example, Republicans from southern states would have high values on the index, while their southern Democratic counterparts would be assigned lower values. In general, the more politically atypical an incumbent is, the higher the score on the modified Ranney Index; conversely, incumbents from states where their own party dominates state offices receive lower values.

My measure of change in style must be further qualified to distinguish between incumbents who need to expand their voter coalitions and those who may be content to nurture an already successful coalition, albeit in a politically atypical area. This is necessary because of the potential within-state variation in the electoral success of political parties: some states may be competitive overall, but regional variation within the state creates pockets of electoral safety for one party or the other. For instance, Illinois may be considered a competitive state, but if you were a Democrat from Cook County you would be fairly well assured of victory at every election. Similarly, Illinois Republicans would be a lot safer in the southern part of the state than they would be in Cook County. Further, even members who represent politically atypical districts can be expected to gain some measure of electoral safety after several terms of office. For these reasons, I have added an indicator of marginality to my interaction term to reflect whether or not the previous election was won by less than 55 percent of the two-party vote.

The theoretical rationale for the inclusion of this term is that it incorporates the notion of the marginal district directly into the measurement of political atypicality. Incumbents from atypical areas with a precarious electoral hold on their districts certainly qualify as an electorally marginal group. Further, these members represent the types of district that are probably most susceptible to strong partisan forces and trends, such as those associated with presidential elections; hence they should be a major source of congressional turnover. Thus this conceptualization and measurement of change in style notably isolates the subset of congressmen who should be expanding their voter coalitions by adopting or converting to more attentive home styles, but it also captures the subset that Mayhew (1974b) sees as responsible for diminishing turnover in Congress.

Thus I further qualify the measure of stylistic change by including a dummy variable in the computation of the multiplicative (interaction) effect between change in style and the strength of the opposition party within the state. This dummy variable assumes the value of 1 if the incumbent won the previous election by less than 55 percent of the vote, and 0 otherwise. In sum, I combine measures of electoral marginality, political atypicality, and changes in time spent in the district to create a single measure of change in attentiveness to the constituency. The result is a third-order interaction term that is similar in nature to the measure of change in style that I will use to analyze the electoral safety of senators. The interaction variable is created in the following manner:

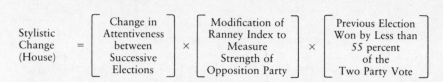

$$
\begin{array}{c} \text{Stylistic} \\ \text{Change} \\ \text{(House)} \end{array} = \begin{bmatrix} \text{Change in} \\ \text{Attentiveness} \\ \text{between} \\ \text{Successive} \\ \text{Elections} \end{bmatrix} \times \begin{bmatrix} \text{Modification of} \\ \text{Ranney Index to} \\ \text{Measure} \\ \text{Strength of} \\ \text{Opposition Party} \end{bmatrix} \times \begin{bmatrix} \text{Previous Election} \\ \text{Won by Less than} \\ \text{55 percent} \\ \text{of the} \\ \text{Two Party Vote} \end{bmatrix}
$$

Since changes in attentiveness on the part of congressmen from politically atypical states are expected to increase their election margins, I hypothesize a positive relationship between changes in style and changes in election results. (As I have noted, incumbents who are atypical of the state where their districts are located receive the highest values on the measure—the more atypical the member, the higher the score on the modified Ranney Index.)

I have found it necessary to apply a logarithmic transformation to the measurement of change in style to reduce the effects of extreme values. This relationship is examined for each election pair between 1964 and 1980. In order to control for the confounding effects of partisan electoral trends on shifts in congressional election margins, a second variable is introduced into the explanatory equation—partisan trend. This variable is coded to reflect the Democratic advantage in national trends across election pairs. That is, this variable controls for the interelection partisan trends that influence election outcomes; a positive coefficient indicates a pro-Democratic change in the direction of the national forces between successive elections.

Table 22 presents the data for examining the effects of change in style on the elections margins of House incumbents. There are two important patterns to the coefficients presented in this table. First, changes in style on the part of atypical congressmen served to increase electoral safety in the House at every election between 1964 and 1980.[5] In every instance, strong positive coefficients appear between changes in style and changes in election vote, and most of these coefficients are significant. Second, there are fluctuations in the effects of change in style on electoral safety. The influence of changes in style on the electoral fortunes of incumbents increased between

Table 22
Change in Home Style and Electoral Change in the House, 1964–1980
(unstandardized regression coefficients)

Period of Electoral Change	Change in Style[a]	Partisan Trend	Intercept	Multiple R	N
1964–1966	2.38[d]	−9.63[b]	17.85	.38	197
1966–1968	2.06[e]	−1.65	1.77	.10	211
1968–1970	3.99[b]	7.60[b]	−10.60	.36	222
1970–1972	3.27[d]	−3.18[d]	4.29	.17	203
1972–1974	4.47[c]	14.12[b]	−24.10	.50	187
1974–1976	2.49[d]	−8.02[b]	11.85	.37	196
1976–1978	4.71[c]	−8.12[b]	14.82	.28	219
1978–1980	1.94[e]	−2.66[b]	2.43	.13	270

a. Change in style has been logged: Log_{10}.
b. .01 level of significance.
c. .05 level of significance.
d. .10 level of significance.
e. .2 level of significance.

1968 and 1974; with one exception (1976–1978), the influence of changes in attentiveness on the electoral safety of congressmen declines after 1974.[6] Specifically, the unstandardized regression coefficients change from 2.06 for the 1966–1968 election pair to 3.99 for the 1968–1970 election pair; the coefficients decline from 4.47 for the 1972–1974 election pair to 2.49 for the following election pair (1974–1976). In short, the effects of change in style on electoral safety appear to be strongest during the period in which perquisites, like the travel allowance, were expanding, and changes in attentiveness were under way.

There is another peculiar pattern to the effects of changes in style on the electoral margins of politically atypical incumbents. Presidential elections appear to diminish the influence of changes in attention in enhancing electoral safety. This alternating rhythm persists throughout the election series: the influence of change in style is weaker in the presidential election years and stronger during midterm contests. During midterm elections, changes in style on the part of atypical congressmen have their greatest impact in promoting electoral safety. The influence of presidential elections in mobilizing opposition party supporters means that these atypical incumbents are constantly rebuilding their voter coalitions. The effort seems worthwhile, if the magnitude of the changes in their reelection margins between presidential and midterm elections is any indication. While the short-term partisan forces associated with presidential elections make the efforts of atypical congressmen all the more difficult, this marginal subset still appear to increase their election margins by increasing their levels of attention. The continued ability of such atypical incumbents to enhance their electoral safety helps to explain why turnover in the House has declined along with marginal congressional districts.[7]

Electoral Safety in the Senate

The analysis of electoral change in the Senate is not as neatly executed as in the House because of the staggering of the Senate electoral cycle, the limited number of senators for whom there is complete data, and the changes in the travel allocation across the terms of senators. My analysis of Senate electoral safety is also simpler and more limited than my study of electoral safety among congressmen to avoid torturing these data; to do otherwise would only produce extremely questionable findings. For these reasons, the findings about Senate electoral safety may not seem as convincing as the relationship among House incumbents. I would probably agree with this contention. Like the drunken man looking for his car keys blocks away from where he dropped them because the light is better, I analyze senate elections only in the "lighted areas." I realize that the darker areas may conceal the most interesting findings, but I feel that more can be gained by looking where one can see "something" than by ignoring the entire question because it falls into the shadows of knowledge. The fact that my findings about electoral safety in the Senate tend to parallel my conclusions about safety in the House will, I hope, make my argument more compelling.

An important parallel between House and Senate elections is the electoral advantage of incumbency. A variety of studies have demonstrated that House incumbents maintain an electoral advantage in congressional races (Erikson, 1971 and 1972; Mayhew, 1974b; Ferejohn, 1977; Fiorina, 1977; Parker, 1980b), and there is also evidence that Senate incumbents have enjoyed an increased electoral advantage during past decades. For instance, Warren Kostroski reports that "the importance of party has undergone a sharp, secular decline, while the importance of incumbency has experienced an almost commensurate increase" (Kostroski, 1973, p. 1229). This conclusion remains unchanged when reexamined a decade later. "Although the incumbency effect may be less in the Senate, it has continued the postwar trend of eroding party ties which Kostroski (1973) noted" (Bullock and Scicchitano, 1982, p. 486). The trend in the electoral safety of senators, however, appears to be limited to northerners since the number of safe southern Senate seats has actually declined (Table 23).

If one disaggregates the data on safe northern Senate seats by political party, it is evident that the shift in electoral safety (i.e., the number of seats won by at least 60 percent of the vote) has occurred primarily among Democrats; safe Republican seats remain fairly con-

Table 23
Senate Elections Won by 60 Percent of the Vote, 1944–1978

Election Period	Percentage of Incumbents Reelected with at least 60 Percent of the Major Party Vote		
	South	North	Total
1944–1948	100.0	22.9	39.3
1950–1954	100.0	18.3	35.5
1956–1960	95.5	24.2	42.9
1962–1966	70.0	36.4	44.2
1968–1972	71.4	38.3	44.6
1974–1978	57.1	37.5	41.4

Source: Ornstein et al., 1982, p. 51.

stant throughout the 1946–1980 period (Table 24). Specifically, between 1946 and 1962, Democrats averaged 5 safe seats while Republicans averaged about 7 over the three election triplets. This pattern is dramatically altered by northern Democratic senators after 1964: the average number of safe Democratic seats increases to about 16 while the average number of safe Republican seats shows no change over the last three election triplets. The changes in the electoral safety of northern Democrats appear to follow the changes in Senate travel allowances and attentiveness to the state: the growth in electoral safety occurs while travel allowances and other perquisites were increasing and declines (in absolute number) after the last increase in the Senate travel allowance.

Since there are no systematic differences in the amount of time that northern Democratic and Republican senators spend in their states, differentials in attentiveness between Democrats and Republicans cannot explain these changes. One might speculate that the increased attentiveness of northern Democratic and Republican senators during the period of this analysis served different aims: Democratic senators may have exploited their attentiveness to their states

Table 24
Safe Democratic and Republican Senate Seats in Northern States, 1946–1980

Election Period	Number of Safe[a] Democratic Senators	Percentage of Winning Incumbents	Number of Safe[a] Republican Senators	Percentage of Winning Incumbents
1946–50	3	9	7	22
1952–56	2	4	10	20
1958–62	10	20	5	10
1964–68	17	30	9	16
1970–74	16	30	6	11
1976–80	14	41	6	18

Sources: Guide to U.S. Elections (Washington, D.C.: Congressional Quarterly, 1975), pp. 485–509; Congressional Quarterly Almanac, vols. 32–36.
a. Senators winning by at least 60 percent of the major party vote.

to enlarge their existing electoral coalitions, while attentive Republican senators may have sought to solidify existing levels of electoral support. Thus liberal Democrats who represent states with contrasting ideological (conservative) and partisan (Republican) traditions may have found it necessary to pursue those behaviors with regard to constituency associated with the expansionist stage for longer periods of time. They could have exploited their attention to their states to disrupt well-established patterns of Republican electoral support and to build successful electoral coalitions.

There is evidence that large numbers of Democratic senators were elected from politically atypical areas during the period in which the electoral safety of northern senators was increasing. According to Kostroski's (1973) classification of states on the basis of the interparty competition for state offices, a large number of the northern Democratic senators who ran for (at least) a third term between 1970 and 1980 represented states with electoral histories that favored the Republican party (e.g., Wisconsin, Wyoming, North Dakota, New Hampshire, California, Connecticut, and Utah). Further, the northern Democrats who were elected to the Senate in the late 1950s and early 1960s represented an unusually large influx of liberals (Foley, 1980). Thus I expect that the increases in perquisites like the travel allowance promoted the conversion of northern Democratic senators to greater attentiveness, and that this shift enhanced their electoral safety.

Since significant aggregate changes in attentiveness to the state subsided as the 1970s progressed, it can be expected that whatever electoral benefits flow from the conversion of northern Democratic senators to greater attentiveness should also dissipate if these changes in home style account for changed electoral fortunes. That is, changes in attentiveness are less significant after the 1973–1974 period, and hence changes in election margins should be less affected by changes in attentiveness after 1974. Changes in attentiveness to the state are confined to the 1965–1974 period, and it is expected that they will be accompanied by increases in election margins during this period. As home styles adjust to the increased opportunities for attention and changes in attentiveness subside, one can expect the effects of attentiveness on election margins also to decline in magnitude.

I test this hypothesis by examining the correlation between

changes in the time spent by senators in their states during successive terms and changes in their election margins. The elections are collapsed into triplets to ensure that every state will have held both of its senate elections during any single period. Therefore, election period comparisons should not be biased because of the particular set of states with elections at any particular point in the staggered Senate election cycle. The election triplets that can be constructed from these data for the purpose of testing this hypothesis are: 1964–1968, 1970–1974, and 1976–1980.

The changes in the time spent between successive elections in the 1964–1968 and 1970–1974 periods (Period I) should increase election margins because these periods encompass the years during which significant changes were occuring in levels of attentiveness. Since such changes are less significant after 1975, I do not expect changes in style during this period, 1970–1974 and 1976–1980 (Period II), to exercise a strong influence on electoral safety. In sum, I expect electoral change to respond to changes in attentiveness during Period I (1964–1968 and 1970–1974), but less so in Period II, when changes in style subside.

I examine this relationship within different subsets of senators to control for possible confounding effects such as those associated with regional, partisan, or national trends across election periods.[8] Because of the limited universe of cases (senators) for which there is complete data, I test the hypothesized relationship between attentiveness and election margins by examining the magnitude and statistical significance of the Pearson product-moment correlation coefficient (r) between changes in attention to the state and reelection margins.[9] The appropriate correlations are displayed in Table 25, which represents the relationship between changes in attentiveness on the part of senators who have served at least two consecutive terms and changes in election margins between 1964–1968 and 1970–1974 (Period I), and between 1970–1974 and 1976–1980 (Period II). I suggest caution in interpreting these correlations since most of the relationships are based upon a small number of observations; I have provided levels of statistical significance to aid in evaluating the findings.

At first glance, these findings provide little evidence that changes in attention had a positive influence on the aggregate electoral safety of senators. With the exception of northern Democrats, changes in

Table 25
Change in Home Style and Electoral Change in the Senate, 1964–1980[a]

Subset of Senators	Period I[b] Change in Attentiveness (1964–1968 and 1970–1974)	Period II[c] No Change in Attentiveness (1970–1974 and 1976–1980)
All	-.32[d] (34)	n.s.
Northern	-.28[e] (27)	n.s.
Southern	-.81[f] (7)	-.63[e] (6)
Democrats	-.33[e] (22)	n.s.
Republicans	-.43[e] (12)	-.51[e] (10)
Northern Republicans	-.37[e] (10)	-.58[e] (7)
Northern Democrats	n.s.	n.s.
Southern Democrats	-.83[d] (5)	-.87[e] (3)
Interaction effect: Changes in style by northern Democrats	.33[d] (34)	.19[e] (33)

a. These coefficients are correlations.
b. All senators elected before 1964.
c. All senators elected before 1970.
d. .05 level of significance.
e. .10 level of significance.
f. .01 level of significance.
n.s. is nonsignificant relationship >.2 level of significance.

attention are negatively related to election margins in every subset of
senators: northern, southern,[10] Republican, and southern Democratic
senators appear to have gained relatively little positive value from
their adoption of more attentive home styles (Table 24). Contrary to
this pattern of negative correlations, the relationship among northern
Democrats is insignificant. The near-zero relationship between
changes in attention and electoral safety among northern Democrats
exhibits symptoms of statistical interaction: the strength of the association between two variables varies according to one or more control variables. This suggests that the relationship between attentiveness and electoral change may vary according to both party and
region. Specifically, changes in style on the part of northern Democrats may have had a different impact on election margins than those
of northern Republicans or southern Democrats.

One can capture the effects of changes in attentiveness on the
part of northern Democratic senators by constructing a third-order
interaction term:

$$\begin{matrix} \text{Stylistic} \\ \text{Change} \\ \text{(Senate)} \end{matrix} = \left[\text{Region} \right] \times \left[\text{Incumbent's Party} \right] \times \left[\begin{matrix} \text{Change in Attentiveness} \\ \text{between Successive} \\ \text{Elections} \end{matrix} \right]$$

In this formulation, region is coded 1 for northern senators and 0 for
others, party is coded 1 for Democrats and 0 otherwise, and the
change in attentiveness is again measured as the difference in the
number of days spent in the state between successive elections. Statistical interaction exists when the slope of the relationship between the
dependent variable (change in reelection margins) and the independent variable (change in state attention) shifts according to the categories or levels of other variables (party and region). Thus the relationship between attentiveness and reelection margins is presumed to
differ according to whether the senator is a northern Democrat or
not. I expect changes in the attentiveness of northern Democrats to
increase election margins in successive elections between 1964–1968
and 1970–1974 (Period I) but to have less effect on shifts in election
margins after 1974 (Period II).

It is clear from Table 25 (bottom) that changes in attentiveness on the part of northern Democrats helped to increase Senate election margins between 1964 and 1974 (Period I), but the relationship declined between 1975 and 1980 (Period II).[11] A logarithmic transformation of changes in attentiveness reduces the effects of outliers and indicates that shifts in attention explain about 25 percent of the variation in the changes in the election margins of senators between 1964 and 1974 ($r = .50$ alpha$<.01$); the untransformed variable is presented in Table 25. I should also point out that both the slope (unstandardized regression coefficient) and correlation decline after the 1964–1974 election period: the slope declines from $b = .03$ (Period I) to $b = .01$ (Period II).[12] In sum, changes in style on the part of northern Democrats could have promoted aggregate shifts in the electoral safety of the Senate during the 1960s and 1970s, since this group accounts for the growth in electoral safety among senators. This is not to deny that other forces were also at work; it is argued only that the changes in style on the part of atypical senators should not be ignored in fashioning explanations for the general shift over time in the electoral safety of senators.

The limited number of senators available for analysis allows a closer look at this select group of northerners (i.e., those who increased their election margins between 1964 and 1974). Table 26 lists the northern senators who qualified for analysis during the 1964–1974 period; it also contains information about the changes in the number of days spent in the state in successive terms and the changes in reelection margins in successive elections. The question here is whether those northern Democrats who were increasing their election margins were, in fact, representing areas that were quite electorally competitive or hostile.

I have organized these northern Democratic senators according to their level of electoral change: senators at the top of Table 26 have the greatest levels of electoral change, whereas those at the bottom experienced declines in their reelection margins during the same period. Austin Ranney (1976) classified a state as competitive for Democratic officeholders if it ranked higher than 20th in terms of Democratic domination of state elections between 1962 and 1973. This distinction and the comparison of the average electoral gain for senators from competitive areas (ranks above 20) with that achieved by those from less competitive areas (ranks less than 20) reveal that

Table 26
Northern Democrats in the Analysis of Electoral Change in the Senate

Senator	State	Interparty Competition Rank[a]	Change in Days	Change in Election Margin
William Proxmire	Wisconsin	37	94	18%[b]
Henry Jackson	Washington	27	105	10
Robert Byrd	West Virginia[c]	18	56	10
Abraham Ribicoff	Connecticut	24	286	9
Howard Cannon	Nevada	21	100	8
Jennings Randolph	West Virginia[c]	18	10	7
Quentin Burdick	North Dakota	44	189	4
Thomas McIntyre	New Hampshire	43	184	3
Gale McGee	Wyoming	50	109	2
Gaylord Nelson	Wisconsin	37	163	0
Lee Metcalf	Montana	25	160	− 1
Daniel Inouye	Hawaii[c]	13	251	− 1
Frank Moss	Utah	34	84	− 1
Frank Church	Idaho	45	188	− 4
Vance Hartke	Indiana	38	29	− 4
Edmund Muskie	Maine	41	110	− 5
Albert Gore	Tennessee[c]	11	155	− 6
Claiborne Pell	Rhode Island[c]	19	180	−14

a. These rankings are in terms of the Democratic control of state elective offices; the higher the rank, the less pro-Democratic the area. These rankings are for the period 1962–1973 (Ranney, 1976).

b. Ranked from largest to smallest changes in election margins in successive elections between 1964 and 1974.

c. State that is relatively safe for Democrats (i.e., rank less than 20).

the electoral gains during this period were largely due to the efforts of senators from more competitive areas. Between 1964 and 1974, these senators increased their reelection margins by an average of 3 percent, while those from safer Democratic areas were losing about 1 percent.

This relationship supports my contention that the growth in Senate electoral safety can be attributed to the behavior of northern Democratic senators from competitive areas. The data in the table also support another element of my argument: incumbents from safer areas gain less electorally from the conversion to more attentive home styles than those from more competitive areas. For example, with similar levels of change in home style, Claiborne Pell lost 14 percentage points in his successive reelections between 1964 and 1974, while Thomas McIntyre gained 3 percentage points in his successive reelections. I realize that these are rather broad generalizations based upon a small, and arguably unrepresentative, group of senators and that there are plenty of anomalies in the data. Nonetheless, the pattern among northern senators is consistent with my argument and enhances confidence that changes in style on the part of politically atypical senators increased electoral safety in the Senate.

Thus changes in the attentiveness of northern Democratic senators—senators atypical of the areas they represented—served to increase electoral safety in the Senate between 1964 and 1974, and a similar relationship appears in the analysis of the electoral safety of House incumbents.[13] In conclusion, changes in home style among atypical congressmen and senators enabled them to increase their electoral safety at about the same time, and with similar resources. This ability is persuasive evidence of the electoral advantage of attentive home styles.

CONCLUSIONS

Popularity is critical to the electoral fortunes of House and Senate incumbents, and an attentive home style is one of the best ways to enhance one's popularity among constituents. By focusing constituents' attention on their service to the state or district, incumbents are able to maintain (and boost) their popularity. Attentiveness to the constituency is salient to voters, and such images carry a positive valence. This means that an attentive style is likely to impress voters. Policy stands, on the other hand, may alienate as many constituents as they please. In addition to placing incumbents in a favorable light, attentive styles are useful for expanding electoral coalitions. This is evidenced by the fact that atypical senators and congressmen who increased their levels of attention to their constituencies were able to increase their reelection margins between 1964 and 1980. The consequence was an aggregate shift in the electoral safety of House and Senate incumbents.

I should also point out that there are limits to the effects of changes in attentiveness. For one thing, there are physical limits to the amount of time that can be devoted to constituency affairs. Members can do only so much for their constituents. While Congress has enabled members to do more by permitting them to transfer some costs, it may be that they are approaching that limit. The size of the task of managing an office grows with the size of the staff. Incumbents generally want to be totally in charge of matters around their offices, but as these tasks expand along with the assistance necessary to execute them, the ability of members to exercise control over their enterprises diminishes. Second, there may be effective limits to the size of the coalition that can be maintained. While it is theoretically possible for members to increase their reelection margins until there is not opposition to their reelection, such situations are rare. At the very least, unusual effort is required to elicit the suport of the opposition party's strongest supporters. Further, the addition of one partner to the coalition may result in defections by others. In any case, there are certainly diminishing returns to increasing one's voter coalition, and there are probably effective limits to the size of the voter coalition that can be successfully managed by an incumbent.

Finally, changes in attention may also have limits. Change in home style may help to attract supporters up to a certain level. For example, even politically atypical House members who received at least 60 percent of the vote in their last election gain very little from further changes in attention. Changes in style may be useful in enlarging one's coalition to a certain point, but its potency may diminish beyond that level. Therefore, changes in attention are not an unlimited advantage for incumbents. Within such constraints, however, changes in home styles can produce electoral dividends.

Changes in attention may also strengthen electoral safety without significantly increasing election margins. Changes that involve the maintenance of an already successful voter coalition may solidify voter attachments and diminish electoral insecurity by adding greater predictability to electoral races. Further, attentiveness, while certainly not cost-free, may be a more acceptable way to maintain electoral safety than constantly to follow constituents' opinions; this is especially true of the ambitious members who have been entering Congress over the past decades (Payne, 1980). Not only is the delegate strategy less rewarding for the ambitious incumbent, but there is no assurance that following perceptions of opinion in the district or state will satisfy constituents. Perceptions of the opinions of constituents may be inaccurate, and this may lead to votes and policy positions that are unknowingly antagonistic to the sentiments of constituents. Some stands may even alienate as many constituents as they win over. Attentive incumbents, on the other hand, may buy some leeway to cast questionable votes or voice independent policy stands by demonstrating a concern for the district or the state. In this way they can guard against damaging losses of popularity stemming from their Washington activities.

From one perspective, atypical congressmen appear to reap greater electoral dividends from the conversion to or adoption of attentive styles than atypical senators (northern Democrats) elected during the same period (1964–1974). For example, a change of 100 days ($\log_{10} 100 = 2$) in the amount of time spent in the district in consecutive terms would have increased the election margin of an extremely atypical congressman, say a Republican from the Deep South, by about 6 percent between 1964 and 1974. The actual range of increase in election margins during this period would have been from a low of 4 percent between 1966 and 1968 (2×2.06), to a high of about 9 percent (2×4.47) between 1972 and 1974 (Table 22). Northern Democratic senators who increased their levels of attentiveness across terms by a similar number of days would have been able to increase their election margins by only about 3 percent during the same period. On this basis, an attentive home style would appear to have greater electoral benefits for congressmen than for senators from politically atypical areas.

Viewed from another perspective, however, the adoption of an attentive style is as beneficial for atypical senators as congressmen, perhaps more so. If one takes into consideration that a senator's term is three times as long as a congressman's, then the effects of change in style in boosting the reelection margins of atypical senators are considerably greater. Specifically, if northern Democratic senators had altered their home styles by increasing their levels of attention at the same rate as the hypothetical atypical congressman—100 days over a two-year period—the amount of change would have been 300 rather than 100 days between terms, and reelection margins would have increased by 9–10 percent rather than 3 percent. Since the upper range of the effects of change in style are about 9 percent for extremely atypical congressmen, one might argue that atypical senators gain even greater electoral benefits from the conversion to an attentive home style than atypical congressmen.

Marginal senators may be making a critical mistake, then, if they devote less time to constituency activities and contact than congressmen since the electoral payoffs for senators are similar to (or possibly greater than) those for marginal congressmen. Moreover, such changes in style may be less costly for senators since they have six rather than two years in which to achieve the same magnitude of change. In this sense, atypical senators may get even more mileage out of increased levels of attentiveness than House members.[14]

Finally, it should be clear that changes in attentiveness cannot account for the vast amount of electoral change that occurs in House and Senate elections. However, I am satisfied to demonstrate that changes in home styles are important influences on the decline of competition in congressional elections.

: 6 :

The Institutional Impact of Change in Home Style

The arguments advanced in previous chapters can now be briefly summarized. I have argued that the adoption of attentive home styles has been facilitated by the actions of Congress as it accommodated the needs of its members. Constituency service, political leeway, and electoral safety were needs that could be satisfied through diligent attention to the constituency. While specific needs may vary in importance from member to member, the adoption of an attentive style could simultaneously satisfy all of them, a feature that made it attractive to House and Senate incumbents at every level of seniority. The attraction increased further as the personal costs of an attentive style were minimized by cost-cutting measures such as increased perquisites and adjustments in the legislative schedule to minimize conflicts between Washington and home responsibilities.

As I noted in chapter 5, one consequence of these home-style changes was the increased electoral security of marginal congressmen and senators (i.e., those politically atypical of the areas they represent). Changes in attentiveness also had an impact on the operations of the House and Senate. In this chapter, I explore some of the institutional effects of change in style. In contrast to previous chapters, the analyses and interpretations presented here are far more tentative and speculative because of the lack of data directly relevant for testing them. My inferences will not require any great leaps of faith on the part of the reader, but they are less well grounded empirically than the conclusions drawn in previous chapters.

The adoption of attentive home styles has had direct and indirect consequences for the House and Senate. Since changes in attentiveness were designed to satisfy certain needs or goals of members, one can expect home-style changes to be linked to the realization of these goals. Therefore, one should be able to see some evidence of the satisfaction of the major needs that prompted the change. Specifically, I expect the electoral safety and political leeway of members and the satisfaction of constituents with the service they receive to attain high levels. In addition to these direct consequences, indirect effects of changes in home styles can also be identified; these are by-products of electoral safety and political leeway.

DIRECT CONSEQUENCES

The widespread appeal of an attentive home style can be traced to three factors: certain needs, such as electoral safety, were a dominant consideration for a large number of incumbents; changes in attention could simultaneously satisfy all of these goals; and the costs associated with an attentive style had been reduced. Members adopted attentive styles for different reasons, and the exact mixture of goals probably varied from member to member. No goal, however, failed to attract a sizable and intense group of advocates. The electorally insecure probably viewed an attentive home style as a mechanism for enhancing their safety. Members representing constituencies that are heavily dependent upon governmental programs and services may have viewed the adoption of an attentive style as the best way to respond to constituents' needs. For the politically ambitious, an attentive style may have provided the measure of leeway necessary to further career, policy, or personal goals. Even if members did not rank these goals in the same order, the satisfaction of one goal often enhanced the realization of others without incurring additional costs. As the personal costs associated with attention to the constituency were reduced, the attraction of an attentive home style rose. This means that despite differing priorities among incumbents, one can expect the widespread satisfaction of each of these three needs to be directly related to the adoption of attentive home styles.

Increased Electoral Security

In Figure 11, the reelection rates of House and Senate incumbents are displayed. It is evident from this graph that the average reelection rate for House incumbents shifts by about 5 percent for congressional contests after 1966, and that the reelection rate of senators exhibits a periodic rise between 1960 and 1974. It might be tempting to construe the correspondence between these increases in electoral safety and the periods of change in style as evidence that changes in attention enhanced the probability of reelection for all. I suspect more limited effects, however. The major beneficiaries of the increased electoral safety are those incumbents who are politically atypical of the areas they represent in Congress. Safer members may strengthen their hold on their supportive constituents by adopting attentive styles, but under these circumstances the size of their voter coalitions (and election margins) would not expand. Even strengthening an existing successful electoral coalition, however, may provide incentives for those who are electorally safe. Attentive incumbents can reduce some of the uncertainty that goes along with each reelection contest by cultivating and nurturing the same supportive coalition election after election. This not only reduces some of the unpredictability about the size of one's election margin, but it also enables members to concentrate their energies rather than showering attention on voters who are less dependable or loyal. Thus, in addition to facilitating the decline of the marginal district and the periodic rise in the electoral safety of northern Democratic senators, changes in attention probably strengthened the electoral position of other members by reducing the costs involved in maintaining successful voter coalitions.

The shift in the electoral security of marginal incumbents is also evident in the electoral surge of another group, freshman incumbents, at about the same time as changes in attention were occurring. Albert Cover and David Mayhew suggest that a useful measure of the value of incumbency is the change in election margins between the first and second elections of freshman members. They contend that "running as an incumbent for the first time, a member ought in general to do somewhat better than his or her first successful election effort"(Mayhew and Cover, 1981, p. 69). They demonstrate that House members have exhibited a larger "sophomore surge" in their reelection margins after 1966: the surge amounted to about 2 percent before 1966 but rose to 3.3 percent in 1966 and to over 6 percent in most

Figure 11.
Reelection Rates of House and Senate Incumbents: 1946–1980

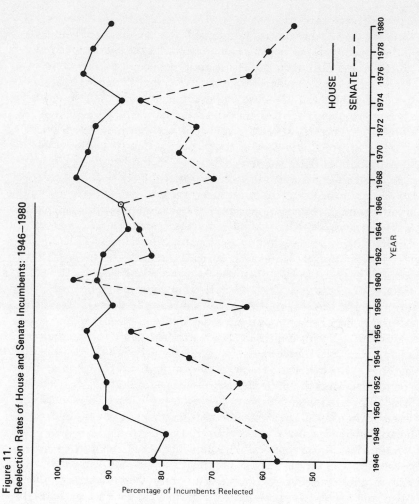

Source: Ornstein et al., 1982, pp. 46–48.

elections after that point (ibid., p. 70). There is also some correspondence between the increased electoral surge among House sophomores and that attained by Senate sophomores. The surge among senators also increases during the 1960s, rising from about 1 percent during the 1950s to 3.4 percent during the 1960s. This coincidence in the electoral safety of House and Senate sophomores and the timing of the change in home styles supports the contention that changes in attention have reduced competition in House and Senate elections.

Constituents' Satisfaction with Services

There is little doubt that constituents have come to appreciate, if not expect, the services that congressmen and senators provide. High levels of satisfaction are consistently reported in national surveys of voter evaluations of members. For instance, over 65 percent of those interviewed in national opinion surveys in 1977 and 1978 (U.S. Congress, 1977; Center for Political Studies, 1978) indicated that they were mostly or very satisfied with the assistance that they received from their congressman. In fact, 65 percent of those interviewed in 1977 believed that neither the congressman nor his staff could have been any more helpful (U.S. Congress, 1977, p. 831).

Another manifestation of satisfaction with constituency service is the expectation that incumbents can effectively resolve troublesome government-related problems. At the encouragement of their congressmen and senators, constituents view them as successful manipulators and movers of governmental action. These images and the reported success of incumbents in dealing with constituents' problems have created expectations of service and successful bureaucratic interventions on the part of constituents. Evidence of the saliency of this perception can be found in Table 27, which demonstrates that more than 8 of every 10 constituents feel that their congressman could help them in some way. What is most remarkable about this expectation is that few constituents (less than 15 percent of those interviewed in national surveys) have actually contacted their representative. Therefore, most constituents perceive their representative to be helpful even though they have never had the type of personal experience upon which to base such judgments. Since there is no evidence that the constituency services provided by senators are any less effective in promoting similar images, I suspect that senators are also viewed as

Table 27
Perceived Helpfulness of Congressmen

| | Year of Survey | | |
Response Categories	1978	1980	1982
Very helpful	36%	33%	33%
Somewhat helpful	46	50	50
Not very helpful	13	14	13
Depends	5	3	4
N	1,715	1,103	993

Source: Center for Political Studies, 1978–1982. "If you had a problem that your representative could do something about, do you think he/she would be helpful?"

helpful and successful in attending to constituents' problems. These perceptions seem to mirror the types of message that attentive incumbents disseminate throughout their constituent communications.

Policy and Career Freedom

It is far more difficult to isolate examples of how changes in attentiveness on the part of congressmen and senators directly enhanced their freedom to behave as they want in Washington. There is evidence, however, that popular images of them are heavily influenced by their attention to their constituencies, and rarely are there any hints of policy content in these images. One has no way of knowing whether this absence of policy content is due to the lack of public awareness of the positions of incumbents on issues or to the efforts of incumbents to elevate other matters, like attentiveness, to the consciousness of voters. It is clear from studies of congressional elections, however, that voters feel that they are knowledgeable about the positions and voting records of incumbents (Parker, 1981c), although they apparently ignore such criteria when evaluating performance in office. Similarly, they perceive their congressman as voting in line with district opinion, whether or not they know anything about the voting record of their representative. In sum,

House incumbents may have some leeway to exercise their individuality in policy making since such activities are neither salient nor threatening to their constituents.

As might be expected, popular images of senators are not as colored by their attentiveness. The differing responsibilities and representational arrangements of congressmen and senators, such as length of term and size of constituency, may make attention less relevant for evaluating the performance of senators. Clearly, the smaller size of the Senate and the broader set of interests normally represented by senators suggest that their performance is judged differently from the performance of congressmen. Robert Swansborough's (1982) analysis of constituents' images in four southern states illustrates the different emphasis placed on service to the constituency by congressmen and senators. Swansborough found that 34 percent of constituents cited the attentiveness of their representative as "something they liked," but less than 20 percent cited that of their senators as something liked. This should not be construed to suggest that the constituency services provided by senators cannot rival the level or quality of a congressman's attentiveness, since few constituents have anything negative to say about the home style of senators (ibid.). I expect that attention to the constituency is less central to the images of senators because they gain the public's eye in so many other (less controllable) ways. Attention provides a positive component to the images of senators in the same way as it generates positive evaluations of congressmen. For example, it is far more likely to make a positive impression on their constituents than either their stands on issues or their ideology. The effects of attention are similar, therefore, for both congressmen and senators. In both cases, home attentiveness generates positive evaluations and may help incumbents to gain some freedom in Washington. They can emphasize their service to their districts or states as a way of diverting the attention of their constituents from those Washington activities, such as voting, that could be harmful to their images and popularity in the constituency. Further, attentiveness can reinforce trust, thus permitting incumbents a greater latitude in their Washington behavior than might otherwise be tolerated by their constituents. Senators may have fewer opportunities than congressmen to divert the attention of their constituents because of their greater media and public exposure. Still, senators possess the same capacity as congressmen to exploit their home styles to produce positive evaluations of their performance and to free them to pursue more personal goals.

INDIRECT CONSEQUENCES

The indirect consequences of the adoption of attentive home styles have been as dramatic as the direct ones. All of the indirect effects discussed in this chapter stem from the effects of change in style in promoting electoral safety and political leeway in Washington. In the process of increasing the electoral safety of members during the 1960s and 1970s, the power in the House and Senate shifted to the northern wing of the Democratic party. This shift had a profound impact on the ideological direction of the parties in Congress and the operations of the House and Senate. For example, with respect to the House, Barbara Sinclair writes:

Throughout the 1960s, as Republicans began winning House seats in the South and Democrats made inroads into previously Republican territory in the North, the center of gravity of the Democratic party moved decidedly to the left. As the liberals' strength increased, they decided to concentrate upon changing party rather than House rules. The committee assignment process and the designation of committee chairs, over which the liberals hoped to gain a measure of control, are within the province of the party. (Sinclair, 1983, p. 5)

The political freedom that incumbents gain from maintaining an attentive home style enhances their individuality. This individuality, bolstered by increased office resources, has reduced the capacity of legislative leaders to command the allegiance of members. Incumbents who can practice a measure of individuality in their Washington behavior without fear of electoral reprisal have unusual leverage with their party leaders. Political parties have few electoral resources to offer their members and even fewer to offer those who are electorally secure and politically independent. The growth of universalism—rules applying equally to all—in the distribution of office resources and influence in the House and Senate (Polsby, 1969) further reduces the incentives for following party leaders.

Shifts in Power

Prior to the 1970s seniority was a decisive factor in the allocation of power and influence in the House and Senate. A variety of norms, such as apprenticeship, supported the power of senior congressmen and senators. While adherence to such norms has declined (Asher, 1975; Rohde, Ornstein, and Peabody, 1985), and the power of the seniority system has been eroded, seniority served to distinguish leaders from followers quite effectively in earlier Congresses. Especially important in this regard were the allocations of power that resulted from positions of committee leadership: rarely was seniority violated in the selection of committee and subcommittee leaders (Polsby, Gallaher, and Rundquist, 1969; Wolanin, 1974; Goldstone, 1975).

The electoral security of southern Democrats enabled them to accrue tenure and gain positions of committee leadership in the House and Senate. As a consequence, they exercised unusual control over their party, its policies, and positions of legislative power. Frequently, committee leaders would use their powers over committee deliberations as leverage in dealing with elected party leaders. In this regard, the adoption of attentive home styles was especially beneficial for northern Democrats: it not only enhanced their electoral safety, but it also enabled them to gain seniority and access to positions of legislative power. As their seniority and numbers increased, so did their influence in the House and Senate. "The Senate's structure may once have been dominated by conservative members, but it is not in itself oriented to raising conservatives to positions of formal leadership. The seniority rule, for example, can cut both ways. As personal longevity and electoral circumstances fostered the conservative leadership of the 1950s, so death, retirement, and defeat allowed liberals with safe seats to fill the vacuum" (Foley, 1980, p. 259).

Raymond Wolfinger and Joan Heifetz (1965) argued that southern control and influence in the Democratic party in the House was due to the greater electoral safety of southern seats. They suggested that the growth in the number and share of noncompetitive congressional districts held by northern Democrats would enable them to gain the seniority and the access to power that goes along with lengthy tenure. As evidence of this trend, Wolfinger and Heifetz presented data demonstrating a growth in the proportion of safe Demo-

cratic seats held by northern Democrats (congressional races won by
at least 65 percent of the vote). In Table 28 the data assembled by
Wolfinger and Heifetz (ibid., p. 347) are extended through 1980.
The trends depicted by Wolfinger and Heifetz continue: the number
and proportion of safe northern congressional seats have increased

Table 28
Congressional Seats Won by Democrats with at least 65 Percent of the
Two-Party Vote[a]

| | North | | South | | Total Number of Democratic Seats Won by 65% | Total Democratic Seats Held |
	N	%	N	%		
1946	23	21	87	79	110	188
1948	45	33	90	67	135	263
1950	38	29	91	70	129	235
1952	28	23	90	76	118	213
1954	54	38	88	62	142	232
1956	40	33	81	67	121	234
1958	81	46	95	54	176	283
1960	69	44	89	56	158	260
1962	63	46	74	54	137	259
1964	106	64	60	36	166	294
1966	62	53	56	47	118	248
1968	42	44	54	56	96	243
1970	97	62	60	38	157	255
1972	82	59	57	41	139	244
1974	114	65	62	35	176	291
1976	128	70	56	30	184	290
1978	112	66	57	34	169	276
1980	82	61	53	39	135	244

Sources: Wolfinger and Heifitz, 1965, p. 347 for 1941–1964 data; Congressional
Quarterly Almanac, vols. 22–36.

a. Some states do not publish the votes of unopposed candidates; in these instances,
   the candidate was counted as winning by 65 percent. Percentages do not total to
   100 percent because of rounding error.

over time. The first real indication of a decline in southern power within the Democratic party occurred in 1964, as a large number of northern Democrats were elected from Republican areas, and the percentage of safe southern seats dropped below 50 percent. With the exception of 1968, northern Democrats have held a majority of the safe seats in the party since 1964.

Northern Democrats parlayed their increased numbers and seniority into positions of influence in the party and in the House and Senate. For example, in 1963, 58 percent of the subcommittee chairs in the House were held by southern Democrats, but by 1973 this percentage had been cut in half (29 percent) (Ornstein and Rohde, 1975, p. 81, Table 5). This pattern is also exhibited in the change in the regional distributions of committee chairmanships (southern domination of committee leadership chairs has diminished since the 1960s). Although the pattern is somewhat weaker in the Senate, northern Democrats also were making inroads into southern domination of party and Senate leadership positions at about the same time (ibid.; Hinckley, 1983, p. 122, Table 5–1). In addition, northern Democrats were making lasting changes in the Senate itself.

Michael Foley notes that the influx of a large cadre of liberal northern senators during the late 1950s and early 1960s precipitated many changes in the operations of the Senate. Many of the members of these cohorts were liberal Democrats who were elected from states with strong Republican traditions. Their ability to survive reelection in these competitive areas during the 1960s and 1970s enabled them to hasten the evolution in Senate practices, procedures, and life.

It was the massive influx of liberals in the late 1950s and early 1960s, however, that embodied the changes in public opinion and precipitated so many of the changes that occurred inside the Senate. In terms of the general life-style of the Senate, it is generally agreed that the liberals introduced "a greater informality of general demeanor and relaxed the stuffiness of the chamber." In the process, the liberals made the Senate a less cocooned and cloistral institution, they reduced the mystique of its introverted and private operations, and they undermined the whole notion of a structural hierarchy of personal status and privilege. Distinctions between juniors and seniors became blurred as the atmosphere within the institution became one of individual assertion. The liberals' disparate ideas and high expectations enlivened the Senate, made it more heterogeneous in composition, and brought it more into the mainstream of national political pressures and trends. (Foley, 1980, p. 253)

The growth in electoral safety also enabled another group of politically atypical members, southern Republicans, to gain strength and increase their seniority and influence in their party. For instance, southern Republicans in the House could claim only 6 seats prior to 1972, but after this election 34 southern districts were represented by Republican congressmen, and many of them remain under Republican control. In Table 29 the percentage of congressional seats that consistently remained under the Republican party's control during a decade of elections are categorized by region. Charles Jones (1964) refers to a congressional district dominated by the same party for a long period of time as a "no-change" district. Using this definition, one can see that Republican control over no-change congressional districts has declined in almost every region since the 1950s. The major exception to this generalization occurs in the South: the percentage of no-change districts in the South and its bordering states has risen since the 1950s. In the 1952–1960 period, only about 5 percent of the no-change districts in the South were controlled by Republicans, but this percentage more than doubles in each successive decade of elections (1962–1970, 1972–1980). Clearly, southern Republicans have increased their numbers in the Republican party, although they still remain a relatively select group; like northern Democrats, their influence should increase as they rise through the seniority system and as their numbers increase.

Individuality and Party Support

As I noted earlier, changes in style had the direct consequence of enhancing the individuality of congressmen and senators. This individuality had the indirect effect of making it more difficult for party leaders to exercise control over fellow partisans. The decline of party as a controlling influence on congressional election outcomes (Ferejohn, 1977) and the rise in split-ticket voting during presidential elections have reduced the electoral relevance of the party for most incumbents. The discretion of leaders over the affairs of their members has also been reduced and has further impaired their ability to offer incentives for supporting the party. For instance, the routinization of committee assignments (Gertzog, 1976) and the development of automatic rules, like seniority, for allocating legislative benefits have made incumbents independent of their party and its leadership.

Table 29
Percentage of No-Change Districts Dominated by Republicans

Region	1914–1926 %	1932–1940 %	Change[a]	1942–1950 %	Change	1952–1960 %	Change	1962–1970 %	Change	1972–1980 %	Change
New England	91.3	62.5	–	72.7	+	53.0	–	36.9	–	35.3	–
Mid Atlantic	85.4	48.5	–	64.1	+	57.5	–	42.4	–	38.8	–
Central	92.3	33.3	–	78.0	+	64.9	–	55.0	–	54.8	–
West Central	100.0	73.7	–	100.0	+	82.6	–	68.2	–	55.0	–
Border	27.8	0.0	–	12.5	+	10.7	–	14.8	+	20.0	+
South	2.1	2.9	+	1.9	–	4.9	+	12.1	+	25.6	+
Mountain	71.4	0.0	–	44.4	+	30.0	–	25.0	–	70.0	+
Pacific	100.0	22.2	–	66.7	+	62.1	–	42.1	–	36.6	–

Sources: Jones, 1964, p. 470; and Congressional Quarterly Almanac, vols. 20–36.
a. Plus sign indicates an increase and minus sign a decrease in number of no-change districts dominated by Republicans.

Party may be an important voting cue for congressmen and senators (Kingdon, 1973) and a useful way of organizing committee majorities (Parker and Parker, 1985a), but there are very few electoral benefits that can be derived from pleasing party leaders. Furthermore, there are a variety of rationalizations that can be effectively used to defend one's actions to the leadership. For example, the claim of strong feelings in the constituency on an issue, whether real or fabricated, is rarely questioned by party leaders and is a quite persuasive justification (Froman and Ripley, 1965). This is not to deny the continuing force of party on the operations of Congress and its members. I am asserting only that party leaders have little to offer their members for following the party's positions on legislation.

The electoral conditions that could provide leaders with a certain amount of leverage do not exist at present.

To the degree that party at this electoral level can organize and express communalities of interest and view across constituencies and play an important role in the conduct of campaigns, party cohesion in the House [and Senate] will be high. Such cohesion, in turn, facilitates aggregation within the House [and Senate] by providing a stable base for organizing majorities across a range of issues and by permitting greater concentrations of rewards and penalties (drawn from both formal and party systems) in the hands of party leaders. (Cooper, 1981, p. 333)

Incumbents have created the conditions that have weakened the legislative effectiveness of their party leaders. For instance, the development of personal political organizations reflects a change in the orientations of incumbents toward their parties, a change fostered by increases in subsidized office resources.

Members now command much greater resources for serving the district. Staffs, office budgets, access to sophisticated technology like computers, and the number of paid trips home have all greatly increased. As party organizations have declined, the local elites on whom the congressman depends for support are less likely to be party-based, and as a result, current members may see their reelection as even more dependent on their own efforts and less so on the party's record than members in the 1950s and 1960s did. (Sinclair, 1983, p. 24)

If party is no longer a dominant consideration in their reelection, congressmen and senators like it that way—separate organizations pursuing different tasks or goals. "The task of the congressman's personal organization is to keep him in Congress. The task of the local party organization is to keep the party in control of local offices" (Fenno, 1978, p. 113).

By being attentive to their states and districts, incumbents have been able to free themselves from pressures exerted by constituency and party. This means that even appeals by party leaders for support on issues that a member's constituency might favor a priori do not automatically ensure support. Party leaders must bargain with fellow partisans for their votes rather than command it. And for many members, bargaining with party leaders is not as difficult as bargaining with the president (Neustadt, 1960); at least they don't have to conduct the negotiations from their knees! Party leaders may have a greater effect on a member's attainment of power and influence within Congress than on reelection, but even here they have only a marginal and a sporadic impact.

One expression of the weakened hold of leaders on the members of their parties is the decline in party voting during recent decades; sharp declines occur after 1966 and continue until the mid-1970s, then rise slightly. The declines (Fig. 12) continue a trend toward less party cohesion that began decades before and that has been interrupted only by unusual electoral circumstances (Brady, Cooper, and Hurley, 1979). One of the most unreliable groups of partisans are those who represent areas that are atypical of their party loyalties.

Members elected from districts previously held by Republicans are particularly troublesome to the party leadership. When northern Democrats first elected in 1970 are divided into those who won seats previously held by Republicans and those who succeeded Democrats, quite strong differences in support patterns appear. Democratic members holding previously Republican seats, many of whom were first elected in the 1974 landslide, are much more likely to fall into the middle less predictable categories of leadership support. (Sinclair, 1983, pp. 17–18)

The variability in party support on the part of such atypical members is frequently attributed to the natural conflicts between constituency and party loyalties. It is equally plausible that the defection of atypical members from the party's position on legislation may be a necessary expression of their political individuality. Surviving

Figure 12.
Party Unity Votes in the House and Senate: 1954–1980

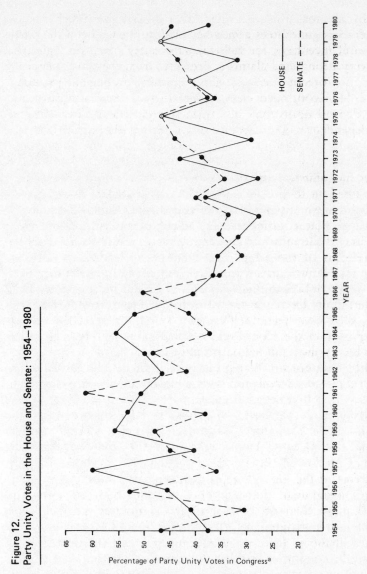

HOUSE ——
SENATE – – –

Percentage of Party Unity Votes in Congress[a]

YEAR

1954 1955 1956 1957 1958 1959 1960 1961 1962 1963 1964 1965 1966 1967 1968 1969 1970 1971 1972 1973 1974 1975 1976 1977 1978 1979 1980

20 25 30 35 40 45 50 55 60 65

Source: *Congressional Quarterly Almanac*, vols. 10–36.

a. Percentage of all recorded votes on which a majority of voting Democrats opposed a majority of voting Republicans.

electorally in areas that are atypical of those represented by most party members guarantees a member's independence from the party: the electoral incentives for following the party's lead on legislation are not very strong, and claims of pressures from the constituency are effective in protecting atypical members from leadership pressures. Moreover, the continued electoral survival of these members may actually depend upon their ability to convince their constituents of their independence—the capacity to go against the party if the need arises.

Pressures for Influence and Power

The freedom to pursue personal legislative goals that members gain from diligent attention to the constituency finds expression in the pressures placed upon leaders for opportunities to satisfy those goals. Some of the most obvious examples of such pressures were the House reforms of the 1970s that made more leadership positions available to relatively junior members and strengthened the subcommittee system. Subcommittees were given greater independence from committee chairs by guarantees of staff, fixed jurisdictions, and control over their own agendas (Ornstein, 1975). These reforms decentralized power in the House and enabled many members to realize their goals of policy and legislative influence.

Another example of these pressures is illustrated by the decline in the percentage of incumbents with a single committee assignment. Louis Gawthrop first called attention to the growth in multiple committee assignments between 1947 and 1965. He suggested that the decline in single committee assignments was due to the "steadily increasing size of most House committees" (Gawthrop, 1966, p. 371). I have followed Gawthrop's categorization of House committees in terms of the percentage of members with more than a single committee assignment during four Congresses between 1949 and 1979: (I) more than 66 percent of the committee members have single committee assignments, (II) between 33 and 66 percent of the committee members have single assignments, and (III) less than 33 percent of the committee members have single assignments. The similarity between Gawthrop's categories and those used in this analysis facilitates comparisons between pre- and post-1965 effects; these data are presented in Table 30.

Table 30
House Committees Ranked by Percentage of Members
with a Single Committee Assignment

81st Congress (1949)		86th Congress (1959)	
Committee[a] Rank	%Members One Committee Assignment	Committee Rank	%Members One Committee Assignment
WM	100	WM	100
Appro	98	Appro	98
FA	96	Rules	83
Jud	96	AG	79
AS	91	AS	78
BC	89	FA	72
II	87	PW	68
MM	87	Jud	63
I PO	87	BC	58
VA	85	EL	48
EL	84	IFC	48
Rules	83	PO	32
AG	82	SA/ST	30
IFC	82	II	30
GO	75	MM	29
PW	74	VA	14
II HA	45	GO	7
UN/IS	0	HA	4
III DC	0	UN/IS	0
		DC	0

a. Committee designations are as follows: AG, Agriculture; Appro,
Appropriations; AS, Armed Services; BC, Banking and Currency;
Bud, Budget; DC, District of Columbia; EL, Education and La-
bor; FA, Foreign Affairs; GO, Government Operations; HA,
House Administration; IFC, Interstate and Foreign Commerce; II,

91st Congress (1969)		96th Congress (1979)	
Committee Rank	%Members One Committee Assignment	Committee Rank	%Members One Committee Assignment
Appro	98	Rules	81
WM	92	Appro	80
Rules	80	WM	72
Jud	63	AS	29
BC	54	BC	19
AS	53	AG	14
AG	45	IFC	12
EL	40	PW	11
FA	39	EL	8
IFC	38	SA/ST	5
PW	30	II	5
SA/ST	16	Bud	4
II	12	Jud	3
PO	0	FA	3
MM	0	MM	3
VA	0	VA	3
GO	0	GO	3
HA	0	PO	0
UN/IS	0	HA	0
DC	0	DC	0
SOC	0	SOC	0
		SB	0

Interior and Insular Affairs; Jud, Judiciary; MM, Merchant Marine and Fisheries; PO, Post Office and Civil Service; Rules, Rules; SA/ST, Science and Astronautics/Science and Technology; SB, Small Business; SOC, Standards of Conduct; UN/IS, Un-American Activities/ Internal Security; VA, Veterans' Affairs; WM, Ways and Means.

As Table 30 illustrates, there has been an even greater decline in the number of members with single committee assignments after 1965. For instance, the number of committees with more than 66 percent of their members with single assignments has declined from 7 in 1959 to 3 in 1979, and the number of committees with between 33 and 66 percent of their members with single committee assignments declines from 7 in 1969 to 0 in 1979. Some of this growth in multiple committee assignments between 1949 and 1979 can be explained by the establishment of new committees like Small Business, Budget, and Standards of Official Conduct, but the vast majority of the increase cannot be explained in this way. It seems more likely that additional seats were created under pressure by members to serve on committees on which there were no existing vacancies.

Louis Westefield (1974) contends that House leaders expanded the number of committee seats in order to manufacture resources that could be bartered for support by members. This is a reasonable proposition; however, if these assignments were not already highly desired by members, their value in inducing party support would be minuscule. That is, multiple committee assignments would not serve the needs of party leaders if members were not already interested in expanding their policy responsibilities. Increased policy responsibilities provided the types of opportunity that members could exploit to develop legislative power and policy influence. As long as a member remained attentive to constituency affairs, these opportunities could be used to further the attainment of personal legislative goals.

Most congressmen may be free to make committee requests on the basis of subject-matter interests, political ambitions, desires for power, and other goals which may or may not be perceived to improve their standing with their constituents. Congressmen may be able to pay proper homage to the Madisonian ideal of constituency interest representation by processing casework, visiting the district, expressing concern for district problems, and making a display of their attempts to resolve such problems. (Bullock, 1972, p. 1006)

SUMMARY AND FINAL THOUGHTS

I have addressed three questions in my analysis of changes in home style: When did aggregate changes in home styles occur? Why did these changes occur? And what have been the consequences of the adoption of attentive home styles? The analysis of the amount of time senators and congressmen spend in their constituencies suggests that a major change occurred in attentiveness between the mid-1960s and mid-1970s. This change was facilitated by Congress as it reduced the direct costs (to members) of adopting an attentive home style by increasing the ceilings on various allowances and office resources and by adjusting the legislative schedule to minimize conflicts between home and Washington activities. The widespread adoption of attentive home styles occurred because such a change could simultaneously satisfy salient needs of members, some of which assumed critical relevance for large subsets of incumbents, and because the costs of adopting such a style were reduced.

Not surprisingly, the widespread adoption of attentive home styles helped to satisfy the needs that prompted the change in the first place. Electoral safety increased, especially for the most marginal subsets of congressmen and senators (for example, those who are politically atypical of the areas they represent). Constituency services also expanded to meet the needs generated by the proliferation of federal programs, and members gained a measure of freedom from their constituents to pursue legislative goals, such as policy influence or power. These were some of the direct consequences resulting from the adoption of attentive home styles.

There have also been some indirect consequences of change in style. For example, power within the Democratic party in Congress shifted to the northern wing as the number and seniority of northern Democrats increased. Incumbents also have freed themselves from the control of party leaders while successfully pressuring them for opportunities to exercise influence in Congress. The political and electoral independence of attentive incumbents and the greater dispersion of legislative power in the contemporary Congress have further weakened the position of party leaders vis-à-vis individual members. Mayhew (1974a) has argued that Congress is structured to serve the needs of its members and to enhance the satisfaction of their goals. It could be added that such accommodations, in turn, can have far-reaching effects on the institution and the shape of legislative politics. These relationships between change in style and direct and indirect institutional effects are illustrated in Figure 13.

In sum, this study has demonstrated that a change in the home styles of congressmen and senators has occurred since the mid-1960s and that this change has reduced electoral competition in House and Senate elections. I have speculated that these changes over time in the styles of incumbents enhanced their freedom to realize personal legislative goals at the same time as they increased electoral safety. The result has been profound changes in the structure and nature of Congress, many of which persist.

While further large-scale changes in style seem unlikely, the adoption of and conversion to attentive home styles on the part of incumbents have left permanent marks on the House and Senate. Clearly, some change in style is still likely to occur as less attentive members (i.e., those elected before 1958) are replaced by more attentive ones. As a consequence, one can expect this generational replacement to

Figure 13.
Causes and Consequences of Changes in Home Style: A Summary

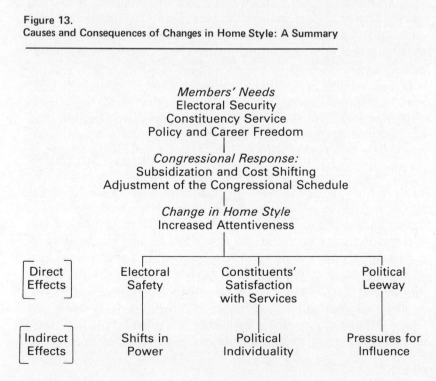

Members' Needs
Electoral Security
Constituency Service
Policy and Career Freedom

Congressional Response:
Subsidization and Cost Shifting
Adjustment of the Congressional Schedule

Change in Home Style
Increased Attentiveness

| Direct Effects | Electoral Safety | Constituents' Satisfaction with Services | Political Leeway |

| Indirect Effects | Shifts in Power | Political Individuality | Pressures for Influence |

boost aggregate levels of attentiveness for some time. Aside from the behavior of new generations of members, however, there seems little evidence that the type of massive alteration of home styles that occurred during the mid-1960s and mid-1970s will continue.

Despite continuing advances in technology that enable members to contact more constituents than in the past, effective limits have been reached on a major component of an attentive home style—personal attention to constituency affairs. Congressmen and senators are spending large amounts of time in their districts and states already, and there seems little additional room in their compact schedules for devoting significantly greater amounts of time to constituency affairs. For instance, congressmen were spending almost one of every three days in their districts in 1979–1980, and senators were spending slightly less than one of every four days in their states during the same period. Can our legislators increase any further their personal attention to constituents?

Even if congressmen and senators are able to squeeze out some additional time for personally courting constituents, can Congress become any more accommodative to the needs of its members for contact with constituents? Congress already operates, at least informally, on a Tuesday-to-Thursday schedule of business, and any additional constraints on the legislative schedule are certain to slow the legislative process further. As it stands, Congress rarely finishes more than a small proportion of its scheduled legislative business; additional adjustments that reduce the time that can be devoted to congressional business will make the task of Congress even more ponderous. The increasing amount of legislative activity (Figs. 2 and 3) seems likely to constrain the amount of time set aside for contact with and travel to the constituency.

Perhaps the most important reason for the improbability of further widespread change in home style is that members, in fact, show little inclination or interest in increasing the demands of the constituency on themselves. For example, 50 percent of the House members interviewed by the Obey Commission in 1977 (U.S. Congress, 1977, p. 875) felt that constituents' demands detracted from what they "would ideally like to do as a Member of Congress." In sum, there seems very little evidence to suggest that another sustained explosion in attention to the constituency like that which occurred between 1965–1974 is likely to occur in the near future.

Even without further changes in attentiveness, several trends related to the widespread adoption of and conversion to attentive styles are apt to persist. For one thing, political individualism will continue to prosper in congressional elections and legislative voting as long as the electoral coalitions of incumbents are dominated by personal followings rather than party supporters; congressional offices often resemble the old political machines of the industrialized cities of the North in their emphasis on serving voters and maintaining organizational loyalty to the "boss." Pressures for opportunities to satisfy personal legislative goals are also likely to continue. One can see some evidence of this in the further decentralization of institutional power. For example, the addition of subcommittees to the Ways and Means Committee dispersed power further within that committee, and the refusal of the Democratic Caucus to rescind its three-consecutive-term rule for membership on the Budget Committee served to spread power further in the House. Finally, the decline in electoral marginality that I attributed to changes in attention is likely to continue, reducing turnover and promoting the electoral safety of the most marginal groups of congressmen and senators. Changes in style may have run their course in terms of widespread and massive changes in levels of attention to the constituency, but the institutional effects of these changes will continue to be evident for many years to come.

Before concluding, I wish to address one final question. What effect has the adoption of more attentive home styles had on representational linkages? It is difficult, if not impossible, to define representation in a way that satisfies all objections or that incorporates all descriptions. Faced with this dilemma, I am inclined to view representation as embodying several components linking leaders to those led. My assumption that representation is a multidimensional concept is not merely designed to avoid defining *representation;* rather, I feel that a multidimensional perspective assures a broader evaluation of the linkages between constituents and their legislators. Of course, specifying the dimensions underlying representation is not an easy task, but fortunately the work of Heinz Eulau and Paul Karps provides guidance. They identify four dimensions that seem to exhaust the various forms that representation can assume.

The first component is, of course, *policy responsiveness* where the target is the great public issues that agitate the political process. Second, there is *service responsiveness* which involves the efforts of the representative to secure particularized benefits for individuals or groups in his constituency. Third, there is *allocation responsiveness* which refers to the representative's efforts to obtain benefits for his constituency through pork-barrel exchanges in the appropriations process or through administrative interventions. Finally, there is what we shall call *symbolic responsiveness* which involves public gestures of a sort that create a sense of trust and support in the relationship between representative and represented. (Eulau and Karps, 1977, p. 241)

Thus one can evaluate the impact of changes in attentiveness on representation by examining the extent to which these changes have altered the policy, service, allocation, and symbolic responsiveness of congressmen and senators.

Policy responsiveness refers to the connection between the Capitol Hill behavior of representatives, such as legislative voting, and the policy preferences of constituents. This is, perhaps, the simplest way in which representation might occur: constituents are represented to the extent that their views guide the policy preferences and behavior of their legislators. Locating such a linkage has met with mixed results, at best. If it exists, its effect is relatively small and selective, conditioned in many cases by unusual circumstances or the nature of political issues. It is difficult to see how changes in attention can do anything but weaken further the policy responsiveness of congressmen and senators.

Since attentive home styles make it easier for incumbents to ignore the policy preferences of their constituents, change in style has promoted greater policy-making leeway and has enabled members to exercise greater independence in their Washington pursuits. Policy congruence is apt to suffer when legislators are permitted such latitude in their policy decisions. The ability of members who are politically atypical of the areas they represent to expand their voter coalitions (chap. 5) demonstrates the ability of an attentive style to weaken the types of bond (e.g., party identification) that might promote greater policy congruence. Politically atypical members are already at odds with salient attitudes and identifications of constituents, but an attentive style smooths over these differences so that these marginal incumbents survive without subjugating their opinions to the preferences of constituents. Changes in attentiveness, then, have weakened policy responsiveness by reducing the primacy of issues in the images and the evaluations of incumbents.

Service responsiveness involves the efforts of legislators to provide benefits to individual constituents. One of the most pervasive examples of this type of responsiveness is the execution of casework responsibilities by congressional offices. Incumbents have always been involved in performing such "errand boy" functions for constituents, but these demands have increased, creating greater pressures on members. As one congressman noted: "Today, the federal government is far more complex, as is every phase of national life. People have to turn to their Representative for aid. I used to think ten letters a day was a big batch; now I get several hundred a day" (Davidson, 1969, p.101). Although these remarks were made in the early 1960s, they are equally relevant today.

Despite complaints about how constituency work interferes with legislative responsibilities, incumbents continue to devote a large proportion of their time and resources to serving their constituents. One reason for the effort is that the costs of performing these tasks have been reduced by increased office subsidies and the capacity to transfer the costs onto others, such as personal staff. For example, increased staff and district office subsidies bolster the efforts of incumbents to identify constituents' problems and resolve them effectively. In addition, such responsive behavior is essential for promoting the image of an attentive legislator, which is externally validated with each and every expression of service to the district or state. Congressmen and senators realize this, and therefore they are constantly looking for ways of demonstrating their concern for constituents; responding to constituents' problems is a relatively painless way to demonstrate such concern. Further, there may be a multiplier effect to service to the constituency. That is, assistance to one constituent gains the awareness of many more through the judicious use of newsletters, newspaper articles, and general advertising by the incumbent. Hence other constituents may vicariously appreciate the incumbent's service. Since an attentive style increases the member's emphasis on serving constituents on an individual and personal basis, changes in attentiveness have enhanced the service responsiveness of congressmen and senators.

Another means by which incumbents demonstrate their attentiveness to their constituencies and bolster their image as an attentive legislator is by "bringing home the pork" (allocation responsiveness). Simply put, congressmen and senators demonstrate their concern for constituents by channeling federal funds, projects, and/or contracts to the district or state. The "cozy triangle" that has developed among individual agencies, district or state interests, and congressional committees ensures that members have the opportunities, "connections," and leverage to gain preferential treatment for their constituencies (Arnold, 1979). Multiple committee assignments and sizable staff operations are two institutional arrangements that aid incumbents in looking after the interests of the constituency without jeopardizing personal goals or legislative interests. Changes in attentiveness have enhanced the allocation responsiveness of incumbents primarily because an attentive style requires the expression of concern for the district or state, and there is no better (i.e., more visible) way to demonstrate this than to divert the flow of federal funds for the benefit of constituents, individually or collectively.

Change in home style may have its most important impact on representational linkages in strengthening the symbolic responsiveness of congressmen and senators. Symbolic responsiveness reflects the extent to which constituents feel that they are being well represented in Washington. This is, of course, a basic repetitive theme in attentive home styles: the incumbent wants constituents to feel that their interests are being constantly guarded and promoted. The constant assurance that this is indeed so is a message that both constituents and incumbents find worth repeating. The decline in governmental trust during past decades (Miller, 1974) and the similar erosion in the perceived responsiveness of congressmen (Fig. 9) have promoted skepticism regarding the performance of political institutions and elites. The reassurance that "someone in Washington is looking after my interests" seems all the more comforting against this backdrop of political cynicism. Perhaps this is why incumbents never seem to tire of delivering this message, and constituents never seem reluctant to listen. And if, as Fenno suggests (1978), trust is related to the time spent with constituents, then the adoption of attentive home styles has gone a long way to increase that trust. While the enormous increase in the amount of time spent in the constituency cannot be expected to produce a commensurate increase in trust, the magnitude of change in attentiveness seems certain to have done so by significant amounts. Thus the widespread adoption of attentive home styles has probably enhanced the symbolic responsiveness of incumbents.

Clearly, an attentive home style accommodates the basic interests of both incumbents and their constituents. Constituents gain in terms of the personal attention of their congressmen and senators, who in turn gain a measure of freedom to pursue personal goals and to exercise their political individuality. I should also point out that neither the pursuit of personal goals nor the exercise of individuality interferes with attention to the constituency. I find no evidence that either senators or congressmen decrease their personal attention to their constituents as they gain seniority or positions of committee leadership. If a political career cycle ever existed, the adoption of attentive home styles signaled its widespread demise. Since representational relationships involve more than just policy congruence, I conclude that changes in attentiveness to the constituency have strengthened important linkages between members and those they represent. Nevertheless, strengthening this linkage has had its costs: the ability of incumbents to use attentiveness as compensation for policy leeway has undoubtedly reduced levels of policy congruence. This implicit trade-off seems to have the approval and support of legislators and their constituents, if not political scientists. This situation may change in the future, or periodically, as during electoral realignments, but for now both parties to the arrangement seem satisfied; hence one can expect the attentiveness of incumbents to continue along with their expressions of political individuality.

APPENDIX

NOTES

REFERENCES

INDEX

Appendix

A. Univariate Senate Time Spent

Undifferenced	1st Differenced	
ACF (standard error)	ACF	PACF
1. .76 (.06)	−.46 (.06)	−.46
2. .74 (.09)	−.10 (.07)	−.40
3. .77 (.11)	.23 (.07)	−.02
4. .68 (.13)	−.11 (.08)	−.01
5. .65 (.14)	−.20 (.08)	−.27
6. .71 (.15)	.29 (.08)	.01
7. .64 (.16)	−.20 (.08)	−.15
8. .66 (.17)	−.05 (.08)	−.18
9. .71 (.18)	.15 (.08)	−.13
10. .69 (.19)	−.10 (.08)	−.18
11. .71 (.20)	−.06 (.08)	−.21
12. .77 (.21)	.27 (.08)	.04
13. .69 (.22)	−.22 (.09)	−.10
23. .60 (.28)	−.28 (.10)	−.28
24. .72 (.28)	.54 (.10)	.27
25. .59 (.29)	−.29 (.11)	.08
35. .56 (.33)	−.05 (.11)	−.01
36. .59 (.33)	.19 (.12)	−.09
37. .54 (.33)	−.11 (.12)	.12
47. .43 (.36)	−.26 (.12)	−.07
48. .52 (.36)	.46 (.13)	.15
49. .40 (.36)	−.24 (.13)	.06

B. Senate Interventions (1, 2, 3), End of Session, and Time
Spent (1st differenced time spent)

	ACF	PACF
	(no noise	parameters)
1.	−.45 (.06)	−.45
2.	−.13 (.07)	−.42
3.	.21 (.07)	−.10
4.	−.06 (.07)	−.04
5.	−.18 (.07)	−.24
6.	.24 (.08)	−.00
7.	−.15 (.08)	−.14
8.	−.07 (.08)	−.19
9.	.17 (.08)	−.08
10.	−.11 (.08)	−.16
11.	.06 (.08)	−.21
12.	.25 (.08)	.02
13.	−.22 (.08)	−.16
23.	−.27 (.09)	−.32
24.	.52 (.09)	.27
25.	−.28 (.11)	.11
35.	−.06 (.11)	−.00
36.	.17 (.11)	−.09
37.	−.11 (.11)	.10
47.	−.25 (.12)	−.10
48.	.45 (.12)	.15
49.	−.24 (.12)	.04

C. Senate Recess and Time Spent
(1st differenced time spent, N=276)

ACF	PACF	CCF (prewhitened recess) (prewhitened travel)		
(no noise parameters)		Lag	CORR	SE
1. −.38 (.06)	−.38	−12	−.035	.062
2. −.15 (.07)	−.34	−11	.057	.061
3. .10 (.07)	−.14	−10	−.045	.061
4. −.08 (.07)	−.18	− 9	.035	.061
5. −.01 (.07)	−.15	− 8	−.073	.061
6. .06 (.07)	−.08	− 7	.053	.061
7. .05 (.07)	−.11	− 6	.074	.061
8. .01 (.07)	−.11	− 5	−.164	.061
9. .02 (.07)	−.09	− 4	.055	.061
10. −.02 (.07)	−.09	− 3	.091	.061
11. −.06 (.07)	−.18	− 2	.047	.061
12. .17 (.07)	.04	− 1	.048	.061
13. −.10 (.07)	−.05	0	.414	.061
		1	−.462	.061
23. −.20 (.07)	−.20	2	.081	.061
24. .32 (.08)	.15	3	.027	.061
25. −.21 (.08)	−.11	4	−.060	.061
		5	−.044	.061
35. −.06 (.08)	−.05	6	.061	.061
36. .05 (.08)	.10	7	−.061	.061
37. .01 (.08)	.01	8	.038	.061
		9	.043	.061
47. −.19 (.08)	−.12	10	−.095	.061
48. .26 (.09)	.09	11	.192	.061
49. .09 (.09)	.06	12	−.126	.062

D. Univariate House Time Spent

Undifferenced	1st Differenced	
ACF	ACF	PACF
1. .88 (.07)	−.38 (.07)	−.38
2. .84 (.11)	.00 (.08)	−.17
3. .81 (.14)	.06 (.08)	−.00
4. .76 (.16)	−.15 (.08)	−.15
5. .74 (.17)	−.02 (.08)	−.16
6. .73 (.19)	.04 (.08)	−.06
7. .71 (.20)	−.01 (.08)	−.02
8. .69 (.21)	−.16 (.08)	−.24
9. .71 (.22)	.11 (.08)	−.12
10. .70 (.23)	−.10 (.08)	−.19
11. .71 (.24)	.05 (.08)	−.11
12. .72 (.25)	.23 (.08)	.16
13. .67 (.26)	−.12 (.09)	−.03
23. .58 (.31)	−.01 (.09)	−.19
24. .60 (.32)	.22 (.09)	.01
25. .58 (.33)	−.00 (.09)	.09
35. .46 (.36)	−.03 (.09)	−.00
36. .47 (.36)	.15 (.10)	.01
37. .44 (.36)	.10 (.10)	.14
47. .28 (.38)	−.16 (.10)	−.07
48. .31 (.38)	.30 (.10)	.08
49. .26 (.38)	−.04 (.11)	.06

E. House Interventions (1–5), End of Session, and Time
Spent
(1st differenced time spent)

	ACF	PACF
	(no noise parameters)	
1.	−.46 (.07)	−.46
2.	−.03 (.08)	−.30
3.	.09 (.08)	−.08
4.	−.05 (.08)	−.05
5.	−.01 (.08)	−.04
6.	−.07 (.08)	−.14
7.	.05 (.08)	−.08
8.	−.11 (.08)	−.20
9.	.18 (.08)	.06
10.	−.18 (.08)	−.13
11.	.04 (.09)	−.11
12.	.19 (.09)	.13
13.	−.17 (.09)	.01
23.	−.01 (.09)	−.15
24.	.10 (.09)	−.08
25.	.00 (.09)	.03
35.	−.06 (.10)	−.05
36.	.11 (.10)	.01
37.	.10 (.10)	.18
47.	−.16 (.10)	−.05
48.	.20 (.10)	.02
49.	.07 (.11)	.02

F. House Recess and Time Spent
(1st differenced time spent, N=216)

ACF	PACF		CCF (prewhitened recess) (prewhitened travel)		
(no noise parameters)		Lag	CORR	SE
1. −.38 (.07)	−.38	−12	−.014	.07
2. −.04 (.08)	−.22	−11	.001	.07
3. .01 (.08)	−.11	−10	.019	.07
4. −.07 (.08)	−.15	− 9	−.055	.07
5. .07 (.08)	−.03	− 8	−.028	.07
6. −.11 (.08)	−.15	− 7	.029	.07
7. .10 (.08)	−.01	− 6	.061	.07
8. −.15 (.08)	−.18	− 5	−.062	.07
9. .10 (.08)	−.04	− 4	.033	.07
10. −.10 (.08)	−.18	− 3	−.022	.07
11. .12 (.08)	.02	− 2	.090	.07
12. .09 (.08)	.11	− 1	−.057	.07
13. −.18 (.08)	−.07	0	.239	.07
		1	−.295	.07
23. .14 (.09)	−.06	2	.053	.07
24. −.04 (.09)	−.03	3	−.011	.07
25. .11 (.09)	.11	4	−.131	.07
		5	.134	.07
35. −.07 (.09)	−.06	6	−.093	.07
36. .02 (.09)	−.03	7	.057	.07
37. .10 (.09)	.05	8	.056	.07
		9	.047	.07
47. −.08 (.09)	−.09	10	−.085	.07
48. .19 (.09)	.01	11	.077	.07
49. −.05 (.10)	.03	12	−.054	.07

Notes

CHAPTER 1: INTRODUCTION

1. These data are based on Gallup poll surveys (AIPO). The figure displays only the average writing in any one year. While these data form an erratic time series, there are multiple measurements during most of the years. These additional measurements rarely vary by more than 1 or 2 percentage points. Thus the observed change in letter writing appears to be quite reliable. The three major points of discontinuity in the trend (August 1949; January 1950; and April 1965) reflect a broader definition of letter writers: respondents are so classified if they had ever written to a congressman; the other survey measurements of letter writing use the preceding year as the point of reference. The more inclusive definition of letter writing is also used in the Center for Political Studies (University of Michigan) measurements (November 1964 and November 1968). In sum, the trend in letter writing seems well behaved.

2. The permeability of the power structures of Congress is probably the result both of the willingness of leaders to make certain changes and of pressures by members for greater access and influence. That is, the increased access of senators and congressmen to positions of influence and power in Congress reflects the effectiveness of pressures by members and the susceptibility of leaders to their influence. It is almost impossible to determine which factor is more important than the other, or which is causally prior to the other. Whatever the causal sequence, the effect was the same: the power structures in Congress were becoming more accessible to more members at this time.

3. One rather extreme example of the expectation that Senate leaders

should schedule business to accommodate the demands on their colleagues is the request on the part of Senator Clifford Hansen (R-Wyoming) to vitiate (void) all actions on the part of the Senate that were taken while he was away from the floor (*Congressional Record*, February 6, 1976, pp. S1448–49).

CHAPTER 2: INDIVIDUAL CHANGES IN HOME STYLE

1. Richard Fenno has noted a bias in survey reports regarding the amount of time that House incumbents spend in their districts. "A comparison between records I checked and the replies to the survey question in the same offices (twelve) indicates a constant tendency for the verbal replies to inflate the actual figures" (Fenno, 1978, p. 51).

2. For additional evidence, see Parker and Parker 1985b.

CHAPTER 3: AGGREGATE CHANGES IN HOME STYLE

1. The demands of attention to the constituency are frequently cited as causes of congressional retirements.

2. The data on state attentiveness cover the period 1959–1980; the data on district attentiveness cover the period 1963–1980.

3. There has been rather remarkable turnover in the House during the 1970s: as of the 97th Congress (1981–1982), about one-half of the congressmen (47 percent) have served fewer than four terms.

4. For instance, if the amount of time that incumbents spend in their constituencies increases rather than declines, then one can dismiss the possibility of aging or seniority effects.

5. There are small (insignificant) differences between the magnitudes of the r^2 and eta-squared statistics for the ANOVA tests.

6. The data for the years 1970–1976 were initially coded in terms of the number of weeks in which members spent two or more days in their constituency. Since most district travel occurs during the weekend, I have converted the weeks that members have spent in their districts into days by multiplying by four (days). This is done because Friday-to-Monday stays would translate into four days spent in the district: members are given credit for being in their constituencies on both the day of arrival and the day of departure.

7. The electoral significance of attention to the constituency was a lesson subject to formal as well as informal transmission. For instance, Fiorina (1977, p. 55) points out parenthetically that the electoral value of constituency service was a theme emphasized in the orientation sessions for new House members that were organized and conducted by the congressional party leadership.

8. This generalization is based upon comparisons between the longitu-

dinal differences in mean attention during consecutive Congresses and the maximum cross-sectional difference (i.e., difference in mean attention between oldest and youngest congressional cohorts) at each Congress. For example, the longitudinal difference between mean levels of attention in 1967–1968 (84.8 days) and 1969–1970 (107.4 days) was 22.6 days. The cross-sectional difference between the oldest (97.9 days) and youngest (113.3 days) cohorts was 15.4 days. Clearly, the longitudinal differences in attention are greater than the cross-sectional ones during this Congress.

9. Fenno's (1978) survey of House members, for example, indicated that congressmen were increasing the time they spent in their districts in the 1960s and 1970s.

CHAPTER 4: INSTITUTIONAL INCENTIVES FOR HOME-STYLE CHANGE

1. At present, members have two allowances: one for hiring staff (clerk-hire), and the other for all expenses previously covered by separate allowances (telephone and telegraph, postage, travel, newsletter, stationery, and general office expense). The size of a House member's official expense allowance is determined by combining expenses from several fixed categories with those for three variable allowances: travel, telephone, and district office rental. The amount of these expenses depends upon the location of a member's district and its distance from Washington. The amount of a senator's allowance is based upon the size of the state represented and its distance from Washington.

2. This privilege was first enacted by the Continental Congress in 1775 to enable members to keep their constituents fully informed of constitutional developments; one of the earliest acts of Congress was to continue this practice. The franking privilege has remained virtually intact, though the law was revised in 1973 to regulate and supervise usage.

3. In 1982 each House member was permitted to hire a maximum of 18 full-time and four temporary staff members for the Washington and district offices. The House also permitted its members to transfer up to $15,000 from unused funds allocated for office staff (clerk-hire allowance) for use in other categories of expense. The staff allowance of senators varies with the size of the state: the annual clerk-hire allowance ranged from $621,054 for states with a population of fewer than 2 million to $1,247,879 for states with more than 21 million inhabitants (Congressional Quarterly, *Inside Congress*, 1983, p. 126). As long as they do not overspend their allowance, senators can hire as many aides as they want.

4. Major legislation, as well as noncontroversial measures, reaches the Senate floor by unanimous consent. This occurs because strict observance of the Senate rules would mire the chamber in parliamentary procedures and delay. As a result, the Senate expedites its business by setting aside the rules with the unanimous consent of its members (on the floor).

The Senate has evolved a highly flexible legislative scheduling system that responds to individual, as well as institutional needs. The system bears little resemblance to what the formal rules specify and rests largely on usage and informal practice. Unlike House members, all senators have an opportunity to participate in scheduling legislation for floor action. Minor or noncontroversial bills are expedited to save time for major and controversial measures. Insofar as possible, consideration of important bills is scheduled to suit the convenience of members. (Oleszek, 1978, p. 135)

5. Recesses can also be strategically positioned to coincide with campaign and election periods.

6. The question arises as to whether the increase in the number of days of recess can be attributed to the increased length of legislative sessions (Fig. 3). As an examination of Figure 6 will reveal, the number of recess days increased at the same time as the number of days in legislative session declined and stabilized: the number of days in session declines after the 88th Congress, but the number of recess days continues to increase after this period. Thus it seems unlikely that the rise in recess days is merely a function of lengthening sessions.

7. The zero-order transfer function is used, rather than the first-order transfer function, because in most cases the passage of the increases in travel allowances predates the effective date of the increase by a sufficient interval to allow members to adjust to such changes. In addition, the publicity attending these increases should reduce the natural delay in the impact of the intervention. Thus I expect the impact of increases to be abrupt and immediate; hence my selection of a zero-order transfer function.

8. Metadiagnosis indicated that a $\Phi24$ parameter added to the noise model was significant. It was excluded for the following reasons: (1) the model residuals were already white noise without the inclusion of this extra parameter; (2) inclusion of the extra parameter did not significantly change the residual mean square (model 2 without $\Phi24$, RMS = 1.362; the same model with the $\Phi24$, RMS = 1.361); (3) inclusion of the parameter did not significantly change the estimates of the impact of the interventions; and (4) inclusion of this parameter introduced a significant spike at lag 13 of the residual ACF for the model. Therefore, the more parsimonious model was chosen.

CHAPTER 5: HOME STYLE AND ELECTORAL COMPETITION

1. Congressional reforms are partially responsible for increasing the information available about the legislative behavior of congressmen. For instance, the behavior of congressmen has become more visible as a result of reforms during the 1970s that opened committee and conference meetings to the public, made committee votes public, and required full financial disclo-

sure and a more detailed accounting of their sources of outside income by members of Congress. The growth of public interest groups like Ralph Nader's "Raiders," to monitor their behavior has also increased the information available about Congress and individual congressmen.

2. The responses that were considered to reference the incumbent's attentiveness to the district were (1) He cares about, has feeling for, is concerned about people, his constituents; (2) He's concerned about representing his people, visits them, tries to help solve their problems; (3) He mails out newsletters, bulletins, communicates through the media, tries to keep people informed of what he's doing; (4) He has accomplished a lot for the people in his state, e.g., obtained federal funds for housing, sewer, water system, business loans, etc. For a description of all the response categories, see U.S. Congress, 1977, pp. 820–21.

3. Attentiveness to the district is a category for classifying respondent likes/dislikes about the incumbent representative. It includes mention of personally assisting constituents, soliciting opinion and representing those views in Congress, keeping people informed about the operations of government, and helping the district's economy. The codes for this category are 321–397.

4. The wording of the question is, "How much attention do you think most Congressmen pay to the people who elect them when they decide what to do in Congress?"

5. There are no consistent positive relationships between electoral change and change in style on the part of all members (main effects), atypical members, atypical members with a previous election margin greater than 60 percent, and safe members from areas controlled by their own party; marginal members are the only group with positive relationships between change in style and reelection margins, but the correlations are weaker and less significant than the third-order interaction term used in this analysis.

6. The sizable electoral effects of changes in attention between 1976 and 1978 probably capture the impact of another large group of congressmen—the "class of 1974." Like other large classes of freshmen congressmen elected in the 1960s and 1970s, many of these members defeated incumbent Republicans; and, as with other atypical representatives, the adoption of attentive styles enhanced their reelection prospects.

7. Richard Born (1979) finds that recent generations of congressmen have made greater electoral gains than earlier ones. This suggests that the findings relating to the effects of atypicality on electoral change may be only confounding the generational component. That is, electoral change and the relationship between change in style and political atypicality could be the result of changes in style on the part of more recent generations of congressmen; this seems quite conceivable in light of the slightly greater attentiveness of newer members (chap. 3). Simply put, newer generations of attentive members may be entering Congress from politically atypical areas. If so, political atypicality may have little to do with the observed electoral change: the underlying causal mechanism would be a generational one. There is no

evidence of this relationship since there are no significant correlations (alpha > .1) between the measure of atypicality (modified Ranney Index) and individual cohorts (dummy variables). Thus the relationship between atypicality and electoral change is not a spurious one produced because of the political atypicality of recent generations of congressmen.

8. It is doubtful that national trends alone could account for the growth in the safety of senators. The relationship between electoral change and party is statistically insignificant during Period II ($r = -.01$, significant at .5 level) and only moderately correlated during Period I ($r = .20$, significant at .1 level).

9. I have eliminated senators who did not file at least one voucher every year during a term, those who failed to serve at least two consecutive terms, and those who ran unopposed.

10. States classified as southern are Alabama, Arkansas, Florida, Georgia, Louisiana, Mississippi, North Carolina, South Carolina, Tennessee, Texas, and Virginia.

11. I have also subjected this relationship to further investigation by introducing additional hypothesized influences on changes in reelection margins, such as prior electoral safety, into regression equations for predicting electoral change. This failed either to improve upon the zero-order correlation between the interaction variable and changes in reelection margins, or to reduce the significance of this relationship (not shown). A more reliable estimate of the impact of change in style on the election margins of northern Democrats can be obtained from the following equation:

$$Y_i = a_0 + B_1 X_i + B_2(D_i X_i) + e$$

where $Y_i =$ electoral change (change in reelection margins),

$X_i =$ change in style (change in the number of days spent in the state during consecutive terms),

$D_i =$ 1 if senator is a Democrat and
0 if senator is a Republican.

This equation enables one to determine if the regression slopes among northern Democrats and Republicans differ significantly. The introduction of the dummy variable D in the multiplicative form ($D_i X_i$) permits the differentiation between the slope coefficients of the two groups. The significance of B_2 would indicate a significant change in the slope for northern senate Democrats. The results are as follows:

$$Y = -.03 - .04 + .05 \qquad R^2 = .20$$

$$t = \qquad -2.33 \quad 2.59$$

Clearly, the slope shifts significantly (t-value<.01) for northern Democrats ($B_2 = .05$) and produces a positive overall slope between change in style and electoral change. This more reliable estimate enhances confidence in the observed relationship and the interpretation advanced. For a discussion of this method for determining the differences between two regressions, see Gujarati, 1978, pp. 295–299.

12. The construction of a similar interaction term for northern Republicans fails to improve upon the simpler partialed relationships: the correlation is $r = -.52$ in Period I and $r = -.26$ in Period II.

13. I have experimented with different formulations of the measurement of change in style among senators, including one that parallels my construction of the measure of political atypicality in the House analysis. Since all of these formulations required greater complexity in the analysis without improving upon the findings produced by the simpler formulation of change in style, I have retained the simpler measurement for analysis of senate electoral safety.

14. Another parallel between the effects of changes in home style in the House and Senate is that the relationship between change in style and electoral change declines after 1974. This decline might be construed as evidence of the expansion-protection cycle that characterizes congressional careers (Fenno, 1978). Even atypical congressmen and senators can be expected to adopt protectionist strategies once they are convinced of their own electoral security. The adoption of a preventive-maintenance approach to coalition building is probably less costly to the incumbent because of the predictability that it provides: they can concentrate their efforts on maintaining support of an established and defined set of groups and interests that have constantly produced safe election margins, rather than incurring the costs that go along with attempting to expand existing coalitions. Incumbents always assume costs when they try to expand their coalitions. For instance, some coalition partners may not be able to cooperate, a situation that creates dissension and the type of disarray that handicaps election campaigns. Further, there is no assurance of support from the groups courted, hence some effort will always be wasted. Finally, incumbents find it necessary to "spread themselves thinner" in attempting to expand their contacts with constituents; one adverse effect of such an expansionist strategy is that some coalition partners may feel neglected as an incumbent's efforts to satisfy become more diffuse. For the marginal congressman or senator, these costs must be absorbed in order to gain electoral security, but for the incumbent who feels electorally safe, there are diminishing returns to expansionist activities.

References

Alford, John, and John Hibbing. "Increased Incumbency Advantage in the House." *Journal of Politics* (November 1981): 1042–61.

American Institute for Public Opinion, Omnibus Surveys, 1947–76. Storrs, Connecticut: University of Connecticut.

Arnold, R. Douglas. *Congress and the Bureaucracy*. New Haven: Yale University Press, 1979.

Asher, Herbert B. "The Learning of Legislative Norms." *American Political Science Review* (June 1973): 499–513.

———. "The Changing Status of the Freshman Representative." In *Congress in Change*, ed. Norman J. Ornstein, 216–39. New York: Praeger, 1975.

Bauer, Raymond A., Ithiel de Sola Pool, and Lewis A. Dexter. *American Business and Public Policy*. New York: Atherton, 1963.

Bibby, John F., Thomas E. Mann, and Norman J. Ornstein. *Vital Statistics on Congress*. Washington, D.C.: American Enterprise Institute, 1980.

Born, Richard. "Generational Replacement and the Growth of Incumbent Reelection Margins in the U.S. House." *American Political Science Review* (September 1979): 811–17.

———. "Perquisite Employment in the U.S. House of Representatives." *American Politics Quarterly* (July 1982): 347–62.

Box, George E. P., and Gwilym M. Jenkins. *Time Series Analysis: Forecasting and Control*. San Francisco: Holden-Day, 1976.

Brady, David W., Joseph Cooper, and Patricia Hurley. "The Decline of Party in the U.S. House of Representatives, 1887—1968." *Legislative Studies Quarterly* (August 1979): 381–406.

Breslin, Janet. "Constituent Service." In *Senators: Offices, Ethics, and Pressures,* 19–36. Prepared for the Commission on the Operation of the Senate, 94th Congress, second session, 1977.

Broder, David. *The Party's Over: The Failure of Politics in America.* New York: Harper and Row, 1971.

Buchanan, James M., and Gordon Tullock. *The Calculus of Consent: Logical Foundations of Constitutional Democracy.* Ann Arbor: University of Michigan Press, 1967.

Bullock, Charles S. "Freshman Committee Assignments and Re-Election in the U.S. House." *American Political Science Review* (September 1972): 996–1007.

Bullock, Charles S., and Michael J. Scicchitano. "Partisan Defections and Senate Reelections." *American Politics Quarterly* (October 1982): 477–88.

Burnham, Walter Dean. "Insulation and Responsiveness in Congressional Elections." *Political Science Quarterly* (Fall 1975): 411–35.

Campbell, Angus. "Surge and Decline: A Study of Electoral Change." In *Elections and the Political Order.* ed. Angus Campbell, Philip Converse, Warren Miller, and Donald Stokes, 40–62. New York: John Wiley, 1966.

Center for Political Studies. *1958 American Representation Study.* Ann Arbor: University of Michigan, 1972.

———. *National Election Study.* Ann Arbor: University of Michigan, 1964–82.

Clausen, Aage R. *How Congressmen Decide: A Policy Focus.* New York: St. Martin's Press, 1973.

Congressional Quarterly. *Congressional Quarterly Almanac.* Vols. 2–36. Washington, D.C.: Congressional Quarterly, 1946–81.

———. *Inside Congress.* Washington, D.C.: Congressional Quarterly, 1983.

Cook, Thomas D., and Donald T. Campbell. *Quasi-Experimentation: Design and Analysis for Field Settings.* Boston: Houghton Mifflin, 1979.

Cooper, Joseph. "Organization and Innovation in the House of Representatives." In *The House at Work,* ed. Joseph Cooper and G. Calvin MacKenzie, 319–55. Austin: University of Texas Press, 1981.

Cooper, Joseph, and David W. Brady. "Toward a Diachronic Analysis of Congress." *American Political Science Review* (December 1981): 988–1006.

———. "Institutional Context and Leadership Style: The House from Cannon to Rayburn." *American Political Science Review* (June 1981): 411–25.

Cornwell, Elmer E. "Presidential News: The Expanding Public Image." *Journalism Quarterly* (Summer 1959): 275–83.

Cover, Albert D. "One Good Term Deserves Another: The Advantage of Incumbency in Congressional Elections." *American Journal of Political Science* (August 1977): 523–42.

―――. "Contacting Congressional Constituents: Some Patterns of Perquisite Use." *American Journal of Political Science* (February 1980): 125–35.

Cover, Albert D., and Bruce S. Brumberg. "Baby Books and Ballots: The Impact of Congressional Mail on Constituent Opinion." *American Political Science Review* (June 1982): 347–59.

Cronheim, Dorothy. "Congressmen and Their Communication Practices." Manuscript. University of Michigan, Ann Arbor, 1957.

Davidson, Roger H. *The Role of the Congressman.* New York: Pegasus, 1969.

Dexter, Lewis A. "The Representative and His District." In *New Perspectives on the House of Representatives,* ed. Nelson Polsby and Robert Peabody, 1–25. Chicago: Rand McNally, 1977.

Dodd, Lawrence C. "Congress and the Quest for Power." In *Congress Reconsidered,* ed. Lawrence C. Dodd and Bruce I. Oppenheimer, 269–307. New York: Praeger, 1977.

Downs, Anthony. *An Economic Theory of Democracy.* New York: Harper and Row, 1957.

Erikson, Robert S. "The Advantage of Incumbency in Congressional Elections." *Polity* (Summer 1971): 623–32.

―――. "Malapportionment, Gerrymandering, and Party Fortunes in Congressional Elections." *American Political Science Review* (December 1972): 1234–45.

Eulau, Heinz, and Paul D. Karps. "The Puzzle of Representation: Specifying Components of Responsiveness." *Legislative Studies Quarterly* (August 1977): 233–54.

Fenno, Richard F., Jr. *Congressmen in Committees.* Boston: Little, Brown, 1973.

―――. "If, as Ralph Nader Says, Congress is 'The Broken Branch,' How Come We Love Our Congressmen So Much?" In *Congress in Change,* ed. Norman J. Ornstein, 277–87. New York: Praeger, 1975.

―――. *Home Style: House Members in Their Districts.* Boston: Little, Brown, 1978.

―――. *The United States Senate: A Bicameral Perspective.* Washington, D.C.: American Enterprise Institute, 1982.

Ferejohn, John A. *Pork Barrel Politics: Rivers and Harbors Legislation, 1947–1968.* Palo Alto, Calif.: Stanford University Press, 1974.

―――. "On the Decline of Competition in Congressional Elections." *American Political Science Review* (March 1977): 166–76.

Fiellin, Alan. "The Functions of Informal Groups in Legislative Institutions." *Journal of Politics* (February 1962): 72–91.

Fiorina, Morris P. *Representatives, Roll Calls, and Constituencies.* Lexington, Mass.: D.C. Heath, Lexington Books, 1974.

―――. *Congress: Keystone of the Washington Establishment.* New Haven, Conn.: Yale University Press, 1977.

————. "Some Problems in Studying the Effects of Resource Allocation in Congressional Elections." *American Journal of Political Science* (August 1981): 543–67.

Fiorina, Morris P., and Roger C. Noll. "Majority Rule Models and Legislative Elections." *Journal of Politics* (November 1979): 1081–104.

Foley, Michael. *The New Senate.* New Haven, Conn.: Yale University Press, 1980.

"For Many Incumbents, Running for Reelection Is Now a Full-Time Job." *Congressional Quarterly Weekly Report,* July 7, 1979: 1350–57.

Froman, Lewis A. "Organization Theory and the Explanation of Important Characteristics of Congress." *American Political Science Review* (June 1968): 518–27.

Froman, Lewis A., and Randall B. Ripley, "Conditions for Party Leadership." *American Political Science Review* (March 1965): 52–63.

Gawthrop, Louis. "Changing Membership Patterns in House Committees." *American Political Science Review* (June 1966): 366–73.

Gertzog, Irwin N. "The Routinization of Committee Assignments in the U.S. House of Representatives." *American Journal of Political Science* (November 1976): 693–712.

Goldstone, Jack A. "Subcommittee Chairmanships in the House of Representatives." *American Political Science Review* (September 1975): 970–71.

Gujarati, Damodar. *Basic Econometrics.* New York: McGraw-Hill, 1978.

Hibbs, Douglass A., Jr. 'On Analyzing the Effects of Policy Interventions: Box-Tiao vs. Structural Equations Models." In *Sociological Methodology 1977,* ed. H. L. Costner, 137–79. San Francisco: Jossey-Bass, 1977.

————. "Problems of Statistical Estimation and Causal Inference in Time Series Regression Models." In *Sociological Methodology 1973–74,* ed. H. L. Costner, 252–308. San Francisco: Jossey-Bass, 1974.

Hinckley, Barbara. "House Reelections and Senate Defeats: The Role of the Challenger." *British Journal of Political Science* (October 1980): 441–60.

————. *Stability and Change in Congress.* New York: Harper and Row, 1983.

Huitt, Ralph K. "Democratic Party Leadership in the Senate." *American Political Science Review* (September 1961): 566–75.

Jacobson, Gary C. *Money in Congressional Elections.* New Haven, Conn.: Yale University Press, 1980.

————. *The Politics of Congressional Elections.* Boston: Little, Brown, 1983.

Jacobson, Gary C., and Samuel Kernell. *Strategy and Choice in Congressional Elections.* New Haven, Conn.: Yale University Press, 1981.

Johannes, John R. "The Distribution of Casework in the U.S. Congress: An Uneven Burden." *Legislative Studies Quarterly* (November 1980): 517–44.

————. "Casework in the House." In *The House at Work*, ed. Joseph Cooper and G. Calvin MacKenzie, 78–96. Austin: University of Texas Press, 1981.

Johannes, John R., and John C. McAdams. "The Distribution of Congressional Casework, 1977–1982." Paper delivered at the annual meeting of the Midwest Political Science Association, April 12–14, 1984, Chicago, Ill.

Jones, Charles O. "Inter-Party Competition for Congressional Seats." *Western Political Quarterly* (September 1964): 461–76.

————. "The Role of the Campaign in Congressional Elections." In *The Electoral Process*, ed. M. Kent Jennings and L. Harmon Zeigler, 21–41. Englewood Cliffs, N.J.: Prentice-Hall, 1966.

Keefe, William J. *Congress and the American People*. Englewood Cliffs, N.J.: Prentice-Hall, 1980.

Kingdon, John. *Congressmen's Voting Decisions*. New York: Harper and Row, 1973.

Kostroski, Warren E. "Party and Incumbency in Post War Senate Elections: Trends, Patterns, and Models." *American Political Science Review* (December 1973): 1213–34.

Kritzer, Herbert M. and Robert E. Eubank. "Presidential Coattails Revisited: Partisanship and Incumbency Effects." *American Journal of Political Science* (August 1979): 615–26.

Landauer, Jerry. "Debates Decline." *Wall Street Journal*, February 7, 1963.

Loomis, Burdett A. "The Congressional Office as a Small (?) Business: New Members Set Up Shop." *Publius* (Winter 1979): 35–55.

McCain, Leslie, and Richard McCleary. "The Statistical Analysis of the Simple Interrupted Time-Series Quasi-Experiment." In *Quasi-Experimentation: Design and Analysis Issues for Field Settings*, ed. Thomas D. Cook and Donald T. Campbell, 233–93. Boston: Houghton-Mifflin Company, 1979.

McCleary, Richard, and Richard A. Hay, Jr. *Applied Time Series Analysis for the Social Sciences*. Beverly Hills: Sage Publications, 1980.

Masters, Nicholas. "Committee Assignments in the House of Representatives." *American Political Science Review* (June 1961): 345–57.

Matthews, Donald R. *U.S. Senators and Their World*. New York: Norton, 1973.

Matthews, Donald R., and James Stimson, *Yeas and Nays*. New York: John Wiley, 1975.

Mayhew, David R. *Congress: The Electoral Connection*. New Haven, Conn.: Yale University Press, 1974a.

————. "Congressional Elections: The Case of the Vanishing Marginals." *Polity* (Spring 1974b): 295–317.

Mayhew, David R., and Albert Cover. "Congressional Dynamics and the Decline of Competitive Congressional Elections." In *Congress Reconsidered*, 2d ed., ed. Lawrence C. Dodd and Bruce I. Oppenheimer, 62–82. Washington, D.C.: Congressional Quarterly, 1981.

Miller, Arthur H. "Political Issues and Trust in Government: 1964–1970." *American Political Science Review* (September 1974): 951–72.

Neustadt, Richard E. *Presidential Power.* New York: John Wiley, 1960.

Oleszek, Walter J. *Congressional Procedures and the Policy Process.* Washington, D.C.: Congressional Quarterly, 1978.

Ornstein, Norman J. "Causes and Consequences of Congressional Change: Subcommittee Reforms in the House of Representatives, 1970–73." In *Congress in Change,* ed. Norman J. Ornstein, 88–114. New York: Praeger, 1975.

Ornstein, Norman J., Thomas E. Mann, Michael J. Malbin, and John F. Bibby. *Vital Statistics on Congress, 1982.* Washington, D.C.: American Enterprise Institute, 1982.

Ornstein, Norman J., and David W. Rohde. "Seniority and Future Power in Congress." In *Congress in Change,* ed. Norman J. Ornstein, 72–87. New York: Praeger, 1975.

Palmore, Erdman. "When Can Age, Period, and Cohort be Separated?" *Social Forces* (September 1978): 282–95.

Parker, Glenn R. "Sources of Change in Congressional District Attention." *American Journal of Political Science* (February 1980a): 115–24.

———. "The Advantage of Incumbency in House Elections." *American Politics Quarterly* (October, 1980b): 449–64.

———. "Can Congress Ever Be a Popular Institution?" In *The House at Work,* ed. Joseph Cooper and G. Calvin Mackenzie, 31–55. Austin: University of Texas Press, 1981a.

———. "Interpreting Candidate Awareness in Congressional Elections." *Legislative Studies Quarterly* (May 1981b): 219–34.

———. "Incumbent Popularity and Electoral Success." In *Congressional Elections,* ed. Joseph Cooper and L. Sandy Maisel, 249–79. Beverly Hills: Sage Publications, 1981c.

Parker, Glenn R., and Roger H. Davidson. "Why Do Americans Love Their Congressmen So Much More Than Their Congress?" *Legislative Studies Quarterly* (February 1979): 52–61.

Parker, Glenn R., and Suzanne L. Parker. *Factions in House Committees.* Knoxville: University of Tennessee Press, 1985a.

———. "Attention to District by U.S. House Members." *Legislative Studies Quarterly* (May 1985b): 223–42.

Payne, James L. "The Personal Electoral Advantage of House Incumbents, 1936–1976." *American Politics Quarterly* (October 1980): 465–81.

Peabody, Robert L. *Leadership in Congress.* Boston: Little, Brown, 1976.

Polsby, Nelson W. "The Institutionalization of the U.S. House of Representatives." *American Political Science Review* (March 1968): 144–68.

———. "Goodbye to the Inner Club." *Washington Monthly* (August 1969): 30–34.

Polsby, Nelson W., Miriam Gallaher, and Barry S. Rundquist. "The Growth of the Seniority System in the U.S. House of Representatives." *American Political Science Review* (September 1969): 789–807.

Ranney, Austin. "Parties in State Politics." In *Politics in the American States: A Comparative Analysis,* 3d ed., ed. Herbert Jacob and Kenneth N. Vines, 51–92. Boston: Little, Brown, 1976.

Ripley, Randall B. *Party Leaders in the House of Representatives.* Washington, D.C.: Brookings Institution, 1967.

————. *Majority Party Leadership in Congress.* Boston: Little, Brown, 1969.

Robinson, Michael J. "Three Faces of Congressional Media." In *The New Congress,* ed. Thomas E. Mann and Norman J. Ornstein, 55–96. Washington, D.C.: American Enterprise Institute, 1981.

Rohde, David W., Norman J. Ornstein, and Robert L. Peabody. "Political Change and Legislative Norms in the U.S. Senate, 1957–1974." In *Studies of Congress,* ed. Glenn R. Parker, 147–88. Washington, D.C.: Congressional Quarterly, 1985.

Salisbury, Robert H., and Kenneth Shepsle. "U.S. Congressmen as Enterprise." *Legislative Studies Quarterly* (November 1981): 559–76.

Saloma, John S.; III. *Congress and the New Politics.* Boston: Little, Brown, 1969.

Schiff, Steven H., and Steven S. Smith. "Generational Change and the Allocation of Staff in the U.S. Congress." *Legislative Studies Quarterly* (August 1983): 457–68.

Sinclair, Barbara. *Majority Leadership in the U.S. House.* Baltimore: Johns Hopkins University Press, 1983.

Smith, Steven S., and Christopher J. Deering. *Committees in Congress.* Washington, D.C.: Congressional Quarterly, 1984.

Snowiss, Leo M. "Congressional Recruitment and Representation." *American Political Science Review* (September 1966): 627–39.

Stewart, John G. "Two Strategies of Leadership: Johnson and Mansfield." In *Congressional Behavior,* ed. Nelson W. Polsby, 61–92. New York: Random House, 1971.

Stokes, Donald, and Warren Miller. "Party Government and the Saliency of Congress." In *Elections and the Political Order,* ed. Angus Campbell, Phillip Converse, Warren Miller, and Donald Stokes, 194–211. New York: John Wiley, 1966.

Sundquist, James. *The Decline and Resurgence of Congress.* Washington, D.C.: Brookings Institution, 1981.

Swansborough, Robert H. "Southern Images of President Reagan, Congress, and Southern Congressmen." Paper delivered at the annual meeting of the Southern Political Science Association, October 28–30, 1982, Atlanta, Ga.

Taggert, William A., and Robert F. Durant. "Home Style in the U.S. Senate: A Longitudinal Analysis." Paper delivered at the annual meeting of the Midwest Political Science Association, April 12–14, 1984, Chicago, Ill.

Theil, Henri. *Principles of Econometrics.* New York: John Wiley, 1971.

U.S. Congress. *Congressional Directory.* Washington, D.C.: U.S. Government Printing Office, 1981.

———. House. Commission on Administrative Review. *Final Report.* H. Doc. 95-272, 95th Congress, second session, 1977.

———. Senate. *Congressional Record.* Daily ed. 94th Congress, second session, February 6, 1976.

———. Senate. Committee on Rules and Administration. *Hearing Before Ad Hoc Subcommittee to Consider the Reimbursement of Actual Travel Expense of Senators.* 92nd Congress, second session, June 20, 1972.

Westefield, Louis P. "Majority Party Leadership and the Committee System in the House of Representatives." *American Political Science Review* (December 1974): 1593–604.

Wildavsky, Aaron. *The Politics of the Budgetary Process.* Boston: Little, Brown, 1974.

Wolanin, Thomas R. "Committee Seniority and the Choice of House Subcommittee Chairmen: 80th–91st Congresses." *Journal of Politics* (August 1974): 687–702.

Wolfinger, Raymond E., and Joan Heifetz. "Safe Seats, Seniority, and Power in Congress." *American Political Science Review* (June 1965): 337–49.

"World of Computers Making a Wide Imprint on Congress." *New York Times,* April 13, 1984.

Yiannakis, Diana Evans. "House Members' Communication Styles: Newsletters and Press Releases." *Journal of Politics* (November 1982): 1049–71.

Index

Allocation responsiveness, and representation, 175, 177
Asher, Herbert, 16
Attentiveness: aggregate change in, 85–89; change in, 30–31, 39, 191*nn*2–4, 6; and cohort effects, 59–65, 80; contextual influences on, 48–49, 51; electoral benefits of, 51, 120–21; and electoral strategy, 51; and freedom to pursue legislative goals, 156–58, 162, 167, 172, 174; as hedge against vote-switching, 133; and independence of constituency and party pressures, 7, 165; limits on, 148; as more characteristic of representatives than senators, 88–89; and period effects, 59–62, 65–66; and personal factors, 53; and political freedom, 156–58, 162; and popularity, 115–21, 147–48, 155; and satisfaction of constituents, 113, 155–56, 177; and seniority effects, 59–62, 66, 68–69; stability in patterns of, 45; as time spent in district, 60, 74–75, 77, 80, 100, 102, 104, 144, 140–42, 188*n*1, 188*n*6, 189*n*9; and travel allowances, 65–66;

and upset to entrenched power via seniority, 159

Born, Richard, 68, 191*n*7
Brady, David, 4
Broder, David, 4

Campbell, Angus, 124
Career advancement, and electoral safety, 22–23
Cohort effects, and changes in home styles, 31, 59–65, 80, 83–85, 88; and congressional behavior, 70–71
Committees: assignment to, 7, 162; independence of House subcommittees from, 167; leadership of, 159, 161; multiple assignments to, in House, 167, 170, 177; and subcommittee leadership, 25–26
Communication with constituents, 13–15, 117–20, 176; through mass mailings, 69, 96; through newsletters, 92, 176; during presidential elections, 124–26
Congress: access to power structure in, 187*n*2; institutionalization of, 6–7;

Pitt Series in Policy and Institutional Studies
Bert A. Rockman, Editor

The Aging: A Guide to Public Policy
Bennett M. Rich and Martha Baum

Clean Air: The Policies and Politics of Pollution Control
Charles O. Jones

Comparative Social Systems: Essays on Politics and Economics
Carmelo Mesa-Lago and Carl Beck, Editors

Congress Oversees the Bureaucracy: Studies in Legislative Supervision
Morris S. Ogul

Foreign Policy Motivation: A General Theory and a Case Study
Richard W. Cottam

Homeward Bound: Explaining Changes in Congressional Behavior
Glenn Parker

Japanese Prefectures and Policymaking
Steven R. Reed

Managing the Presidency: Carter, Reagan, and the Search for Executive Harmony
Colin Campbell, S.J.

Perceptions and Behavior in Soviet Foreign Policy
Richard K. Herrmann

Political Leadership: A Source Book
Barbara Kellerman

The Politics of Public Utility Regulation
William T. Gormley, Jr.

The Presidency and Public Policy Making
George C. Edwards III, Steven A. Shull, and Norman C. Thomas, Editors

Public Policy in Latin America: A Comparative Survey
John W. Sloan

Roads to Reason: Transportation, Administration, and Rationality in Colombia
Richard E. Hartwig

The Struggle for Social Security, 1900-1935
Roy Lubove